TIME OUT FOR THE FAMILY

BY
Bill Maynard

QUALITY PUBLICATIONS
P.O. BOX 1060
ABILENE, TEXAS 79604-1060
(915) 677-6262

ISBN: 0-89137-119-2

Dedicated To

Ruby G. (Brewer) Maynard

This book and the life I live could not be possible without my precious Ruby. She has been a faithful wife to me and a good mother to our boys. Ruby and I have been married for 21 years, and we love each other more each day then we ever did. I cannot imagine going through life without my Ruby. A good friend of ours named Veda Gooch wrote a poem for us "preaching boys" while we were in school. This poem describes my Ruby.

Brave Women

They follow their men as they go out to preach,
They study so hard that they may teach.
What if there's tears and shattered dreams,
A day or two of rain? It seems
Their smile grows even brightier still,
As they think of their work, their place to fill.
They pray that God, new strength will give
In the unknown places where they will live.
May he guide their hands in all they do.
May they always be sincere and true.
And the words they speak, only kindness be,
And their steps, dear Lord, lead home to thee.

Veda Gooch

I proudly dedicate this book to my best friend, Ruby Maynard.

Acknowledgements

* To Peggy Flowers, who graciously gave of her time in helping to prepare this book for publication. Thanks for the many hours of typing and re-typing this book.

* To Ronny Keller for the beautiful art work throughout this book.

* The Bible class that Herdis Kyle and I have been teaching for the past three years on the family. They have helped me a lot in gaining the material for this book.

* To Todd and Chad for the experience that Ruby and I gained while rearing them. We tried to use the material of this book to help them in their lives.

Contents

Introduction

This book has come to exist because of many tears for my family and the families of the parents who were in my class on the family which I and one of our elders, Herdis Kyle, have taught for the past three years. This has been the best class that I have ever been a part of. The reason this class has been so good is because all of us have needs concerning the family, and we share those in this class. Each chapter of this book was discussed in class.

I wish I could give you exact answers on how to be a better husband or wife, or to be better parents, or to even be better children, but I can't. I do believe that this book will help you to be a better person in the family unit. I believe that you can read every book in the world and still not know enough to be a good parent. I also believe that you can *never* read a book and still be a good parent. I guess the answer is to be the best family, and still we will be lacking in something. This book is meant to be used in a class, such as ladies' class, or as we did, in a class which contained husbands, wives, parents, grandparents and children. The questions and answers at the end of each chapter will be very helpful for a classroom discussion. This book can also be used for leisure reading about the family. I know that if you read this book, then it will help you with your family life. I feel all of us need help with the family. In this work on the family, the main point that I want to make is that we must still love our children, mate, parents or grandparents, even though they may hurt us at times. They all need to know that our love for them is unconditional.

Why have a study or write a book on the home? There are reasons for a study on this subject. I have read and researched many books on the home. Many of them are very good. But one reason why I am writing this is to make it as simple and condensed as possible. It is hard to go through a lot of words to find something that might help you with your family. I hope that this book will help to provide you with some of the answers you are seeking concerning your family.

The family today is in trouble. There are many "things" and "peo-

1

ple" pulling it apart and destroying many homes. Outside of the church, the home is the most important thing in life. I don't mean to give you the impression that the home is destroyed and there is no hope. Many are telling us that today, but I disagree with them. I believe that most homes are alive and well. It is just that every home in this world can be improved upon. I know that my family and I can improve on many things. Writing this book has helped me to think of many ideas for my family. I would suggest that you do the same thing. Sit down and write a book on your home and how you can improve it. You don't have to have it published. You will be surprised how much it will help you in your home life. I have already written about half of this book before writing this introduction, and I have learned a lot about my family and myself. If you will take the time to look at the topics we will discuss in this book, I am sure you will find something interesting, plus something that will help you. This book is not one that was just a spur-of-the moment decision. I have been interested in the home for many years. First, I have read and asked others how I can improve my home life. I have been teaching a class on the subject of the home for several years now. Anytime that you teach a class on any subject, the teacher gets more out of it than the student. There are two reasons for this. First, the teacher must read and study a lot before he teaches the class. He will read much concerning the subject that he won't ever use in the class, but it will be stored in his mind. The second reason why the teacher gets a lot out of a class situation is that during the class many students will bring up great ideas and good information on the subject that the teacher missed in his research. This is one reason why I will wait a year from now before I have this book published. I expect to gain a lot of knowledge and wisdom from the class within the next year.

In closing, I believe that this book will help you so much that I would like to make a deal with you. If you don't like it, and if you don't get one thing out of it that will help you, then return the book to me and I will refund your money. That's part of the deal, and the other part is if you like it and you get a lot of information out of it, then buy one for a friend and help their family life also. Okay?

There are many good books on the subject concerning the family. Some are hard to read; some are simple to read. Some will benefit you and some will not. I suggest that you do like I do every week. When you see a book concerning the family, buy it, or borrow it. The price of a family book should never be considered. I have a list of books in the back of this book that I would suggest for you to read and study. They also make great gifts for birthdays or holidays, and I think a gift like this expresses a lot of love and concern.

2

Dating

I am sure that most of you know what I am going to say on this subject even before I get started. If you are not married, then please read this because it might help you in choosing a mate that you will spend the rest of your life with. I believe that this will be one of the most important decisions that you will ever make in your entire life. You might disagree and say that a career is more important. What good is a great career with lots of money if you have a mate who makes life hard for you all the time? The Bible gives us a good reason why we should choose the right person in Proverbs 21:9: *"It is better to dwell in a corner of the housetop, than with a brawling woman in a wide house."* The wise man is saying that it is better to have a good woman and small house, than to have a bad woman with a big, fancy house. You see, money and fame are nothing unless you have a good family life.

Now for you girls who are dating read Proverbs 21:29: *"A wicked man hardeneth his face. . ."* This is saying that a bad man will be stubborn. He won't listen to anyone, and he doesn't know what direction to go in. I hope by now that you can see how important it is to date the right person. Let me suggest some things that you should look for while you are dating.

Life-Long Commitment

When you are looking for a date, look for someone that you would like to spend the rest of your life with. Remember, scripturally speaking, your choice must be final. Look closely before deciding if the one you are dating is the one you want to live the rest of your life with. While dating, if you only look for physical beauty alone, you will choose the wrong person. It is good to look for a lovely person, but beauty isn't everything and you will find that out one day. I have seen some beautiful people in this world who make up a great home. I hope you think that your spouse looks great. The Bible has designed it so

4

that you will be with the same person for the rest of your life. There are only two ways that you can be separated. Read Matthew 19:9 and 1 Corinthians 7:39. The two ways of separation are "death" and "fornication" (unfaithfulness). This is why it is so important to marry the right person. Once you get married it is a life-long commitment. There will be times of sickness, times of hardship, times of no money, times of friends leaving you, and times of bad living. Look for someone who can work with you through the difficult times and help you to remain faithful always.

The Date

Why is it that whenever we think of a date, it is mostly always at night? I believe that it is because that is when we are the weakest and we think no one is watching us. The police will tell us that most crimes happen at night. Most accidents happen at night. With all of this and much more that goes on at night, then young people *please* be careful what you do and where you go at night. You might be saying, "How does Bill know the problems of dating today? It's been 20 years since he had a date." That is not so. I have a date about every Tuesday and Friday with a beautiful young woman named Ruby Gail. I still court her and bring her candy and flowers. Another reason why I know something about dating is that we have two sons, ages 14 and 19 who think somewhat about girls. Then I have another reason why I know some things about dating. Ruby and I have had about 20 foster children to live with us over the past few years. The greatest problems that we ever had with them concerned dating. The worst place was the skating rink. I don't know what it is, but somehow skating rinks cause a lot of problems. I love to skate as does my whole family. When the church has a skating get-together, we have a great time. But when it is open skating, somehow there are a lot of problems. We are fighting this problem now with our oldest son. I pray that he will survive this without getting into trouble. The date is a very important event, so keep it pure and go to good places, not to "hang-outs."

Today there are so many places for young people to go. There are good restaurants, shopping malls, friends' homes, church activities and hundreds of other good places. Just find a good place and go there. I'm sure I don't have to remind you of the danger of drinking alcohol or driving fast and things like that. I'm persuaded that you don't do these things. I can see your smile right now, so let me pat you on the back for being a good example.

Date Persons Whom Your Parents Approve Of

I know you think your parents are old fogies and don't approve of your dates at times. I have seen people who look like angels and turn out to be bums. I have seen people who look like bums and turn out to be angels. I used to say that you couldn't trust anyone who had a beard on his face.

Guess who has had one for six years? I realize that it's hard to choose the right person, but I'll bet your parents could choose a better *date*, and even a better *mate* than you could. I realize that they can't choose your dates for you, and I don't think they should try. The best advice I can give you is to choose a date that you think your parents would approve of.

Steady Dating

This can be the best or worst thing that could ever happen to you. While steady dating, there will be jealousy between you. You must overcome this and enjoy one another's company. There will be more temptation to do wrong things while dating steady. When you feel this temptation is getting to you, seek help from your preacher, parents or anyone who will listen to you. This temptation will be harder on you as the days go by. God has designed marriage to have certain rights. Marriage is the *only* time for these rights. If you don't control yourself, this will cause more trouble and sin than you can ever imagine.

It seems that our minds are like a computer. What you put into the computer will show up when you turn it on. Man is the same way. If we put bad thoughts into our minds by reading dirty magazines or by watching dirty movies, then it will come in our actions one day. While steady dating, or at anytime in your life, Christians should never go to movies with an "R" or an "X" rating. I know that some "R" movies are so rated because of the violence and are not too bad. But I am 41 years old and I don't go to "R" rated movies. I believe that most of them are wrong, and if you are watching these movies with a date, then that computer will put those dirty thoughts into your memory bank.

Read 1 Corinthians 7:1-5, and that may help you on this subject. Here are a few more scriptures that should help. Matthew 5:27,28 and Hebrews 13:4.

NOTE - Before you, or your young teenagers, start to date, have them make a list of about 10 characteristics they would like to see in their date. Example: Kindness, Being a Christian, Courteous, etc. By making this list it will help to keep in mind the things that are important in a relationship. If your sons or daughters should ever deviate from these characteristics, then you can ask them what changed and help them to get back to the qualifications they listed as important. It will be *their* list and not yours as a parent. This might help to save a lot of arguments later on, plus a lot of pain and tears.

Dating

1. Explain and discuss Proverbs 21:9.

2. Explain and discuss Proverbs 21:29.

3. Why does physical beauty blind our eyes?

4. What are the only two ways a person can scripturally remarry?

5. Where would be a good place to find a mate and where would not be a good place?

6. Why should parents approve of their children's dates?

7. Name some things that lead to temptation while steady dating.

HUSBANDS AND WIVES

Husbands And Wives

G od has set this relationship up to be the highest and happiest of all earthly relationships. It is so sad that we don't always treat it as God expects us to. Let us notice husbands first; then we will talk about the wives.

Husband

God has given you the best thing that you will ever have in life. If you stay faithful to your wife, she will be the light of your life. Here are a few suggestions for how you must treat her:

You must love her with all your heart. The Bible says in Ephesians 5:25 that you must love her so much that you are willing to die for her if need be. If you truly love her, then you will want the best for her. You will never treat her wrong. You will never hit or abuse her. A man is a fool who abuses his wife.

You must stay faithful to her. There is no room in your home for another woman. If you want to keep her, then don't cheat on her. If you cheat on her, you will end up in hell if you don't repent of it. And you might end up there sooner than you think, because she might just kill you!

You must always be kind to your wife. Never say bad things about her, especially in front of other people. The Bible teaches in Ephesians 4:32: **"And be ye kind one to another, tenderhearted, forgiving one another, even as God for Christ's sake hath forgiven you."** You will never regret being kind of your wife.

When you were married, your vows were for better or worse. As a husband, you must understand there will be times when your wife will be feeling bad and won't want to do things with you. Have patience and accept it when this happens. There will be times when you aren't getting along well. Nothing in this life is perfect. Work on it and make it better each day. One day you can look back at the bad times and have a good laugh over them. You cannot expect to agree on everything all the time, so accept it and work your problems out every day. Someone has said that marriage is a give and take arrangement. I disagree with that. I believe that marriage is a give and give arrangement. Neither is it a 50/50 arrangement, it is a 100%/100% arrangement. Don't wait on your mate to apologize for something -you do it first. Always give and never expect to take from the other. Try your best to see how you can please her. God has set it up for you to have only one wife, so treat her right, take care of her, love her and give your life for her. There are only two ways you will ever be separated. Those two ways are death and adultery (Matthew 19:19).

I call my wife about three or four times a day, and she calls me several times. We love each other so much that we just want to talk to each other. I hope that you are in a position at work where you can do that. I know many cannot. Try to write her a letter every now and then, telling her how much she means to you. By all means, tell her that you love her day and night. Peter tells us in 1 Peter 3:7: "Likewise ye husbands, dwell with them according to knowledge, giving honour unto the wife, as unto the weaker vessel, and as being heirs together of the grace of life; that your prayers be not hindered." Protect her, and make sure she is secure. A vessel can break very easily. You must make sure that nothing harms it. Protect it with your life. You have a vessel that is one of a kind. There is not, and never will be, another vessel like the one you have. Isn't it great to have something that is one of a kind, something no one else has?

Never stop courting your wife. Take her out to eat. Take her away from the children every now and then. Spend a weekend in a motel somewhere. It could even be in the same town that you live in. Some of the best times that Ruby and I have together are when we walk or run in the mornings before we go to work. We get to talk and smile at one another a lot. It helps us to get started for the day that is before us. Many people will tell you that you need to spend quality time with your wife and not quantity. Well I disagree with that. I believe that you need to spend every minute that you can with your wife. You need to set aside special times of the day to be together. Ruby and I like 10:00 to 11:00 p.m. The boys are asleep and we have an hour or two of peace and quiet. This is a good time for us to read and to talk about everything that is on our minds.

Wives

As a wife, there are many things you must do to help your husband and children. You can run the home better than anyone in the world. Let me mention a few things that might help you do a better job.

First, you must be submissive to your husband. Please don't stop reading because this is not what *I* think, but this is what the *Bible teaches*. Look at Genesis 3:16: ". . .and thy desire shall be to thy husband, and he shall rule over thee." This doesn't mean that he is to treat you like a slave or a dog. It means that he is the head of the home and you must give him that authority and respect. Also read 1 Peter 3:5,6. This will tell you how wives did in the old days. There will be a big temptation for you to find a job outside the home. In this book you will find a chapter on this subject, so I won't say much about it now. If you are thinking about it, then please stop right now. Wives should be wives and mothers at home. This is the highest honor you will ever receive. A wife at home works hard and is the best thing a husband and children could ever have in their lives. So please, don't start a job outside the home, especially if you have little children.

Speaking as a husband, I will tell you a few things that you need to do for your husband. *You should tell him how much you love him every day.* He will appreciate it more than you will ever know. Make him a favorite cake or pie, and tell him that you want him to eat all of it, because it is just for him. Make sure that you see the good things that he does, and tell him about them. Pat him on the back when he has done a good job, especially a job for you around the house. The Bible teaches that the husband is the head of the house. You are not his slave, but let him fulfil his job in the way God has designed it to be.

Husbands And Wives

1. Discuss Ephesians 5:25.

2. What does kindness have to do with your mate?

3. Explain the 50/50 arrangement, and how it should be the 100/100 arrangement.

4. Discuss 1 Peter 3:5,6.

5. Is it important to tell your husband that you love him? and vice-versa?

CHILDREN

Children

I believe this is the hardest chapter that I will ever have to write in this book. Children are people whom we will never thoroughly understand. Ruby and I have had over 20 foster children living with us during our married life, and every one of them was different. I believe that no two people in this world are exactly alike. I have often wondered what is in the mind of children. What do they think of me and of other people? We have two boys, and they are as different as night and day. We love both of them and wouldn't take anything for them. (Sometimes we would *give* them away, though.) Just kidding, Todd and Chad.

It is strange how children can make you so proud of them one day, and the next day they can break your heart. Some people say that once they grow up, your problems will be over. I disagree with that. I believe as they get older, the problems get bigger. I have read a few good books on how to help your children during their growing years. Most of the psychologists who write these books tell us things that seldom work. Plus, it is so far above our heads that we can't understand it. I hope that this book will help you and won't be over your head. I doubt that it will be over your head, because I am basically a simple person, and I want to help you by writing this book. I am not writing this to make money. I don't need any more money, and I don't *want* any more money. I'm writing this to help myself and you. Let me suggest some things that will help you with your children.

1. Church
2. Friends
3. Example
4. Discipline
5. Strong family ties
6. Love
7. Responsibility
8. Working outside the home

Church

I believe there will always be some type of problem with our children. Or should I say, with the parent *and* the child. Parents must always try to work together. The best way that I know how to rear children is to bring them up in the church. Paul said in Ephesians 6:4, "And, ye fathers, provoke not your children to wrath; but bring them up in the nurture and admonition of the Lord." We as parents have a command from God to bring our children up as God would have it. The church is the only means that can help us in bringing up our children. You can turn to psychologists, friends, family, teachers, counselors, etc., but only through the church and the Bible will you get the right answer for your problems. I realize that no matter how religious we or our children are there will still be temptation and problems to solve. Because we are Christian doesn't keep us from sin. But one thing is for sure, it helps us in times of need. In Psalm 46:1, we are told that "God is our refuge and strength, a very present help in trouble." Parents and children, if we all rely on God when we disagree or need help, then don't you think that everything will work out for the best? Now children, you also have a command to obey your parents. Ephesians 6:1 says "Children, obey your parents in the Lord; for this is right." Paul could have said many things about why you should obey your parents. He could have said because they are smarter, older, wiser, more knowledgeable, have more experience, etc. But he said, obey them because it is *right*. This is the right thing to do. If you want to do that which is right, then obey your parents. If you are young and are reading this book, let me suggest one thing to you. Obey God, and everything else will work out sooner or later.

Friends

You can have too much money, but you will never have too many friends. Friends are the most important people in the world. I always try to gain more friends. They can guide you and help you. A friend will cry with you and laugh with you. Whenever you are in need, a friend will always be there to help you. A good friend will be closer to you than a brother. (Proverbs 18:24). Young people, you will always gain from your friends. When you move to another town, you will gain other friends. When you go to school, you will acquire many more. When you go to church, you will form a closeness with your brothers and sisters in Christ. Friends will come and go. Make sure before you choose your friends that they are people whom your parents would be pleased with. It is sad to say, but some people in this life are not good friends, even though they claim to be. They will do bad things and cause you to do bad things. When a friend smokes, you may be tempted to smoke. When a friend curses, that will tempt you to curse. When a friend drinks alcoholic beverages, he may tempt you to do the same. You see, your friends will cause you to do what they do. If you don't want to end up in trouble, then please choose the right friends. Friends can make you or break you. I know that parents won't always agree with the friends you choose, but it is very important to have friends that they approve of.

Read 1 Corinthians 15:33.

Example

This portion will relate to parents and children. Look at Romans 14:16: "Let not then your good be evil spoken of." The Bible and everything else teaches us that our example is more important than anything. Let us talk about parents first. Parents do you expect your children to do what is right when you don't? Do you want your children to lie, smoke, drink alcohol, curse, cheat, steal, gossip, etc.? If you don't want them to do these things, then you had better not do them either. Don't you want your children to be like you when they grow up? Sure you do. You want the best for them, just as I do for my boys. Children are watching everything that we do, so remember Mom and Dad they will also do what they see you do. Look at 1 Peter 2:12: "For even hereunto were ye called; because Christ also suffered for us, leaving us an example, that ye should follow his steps." Christ is our example so we must follow in His steps. Now, young people, you have friends, enemies, teachers, business people, and a number of watching you. You have to be a good example, or you could be ruined for the rest of your life. No one likes a person who is a bad example. Even your friends will get tired of it sooner or later. I am sure you want your parents and those around you to be proud of you. The only way they can be proud of you is for you to be a good example. Have you ever wondered why some people are liked by others, and how some people get better jobs in life? They seem to get the good breaks in life. I believe it is because of their positive attitude. If you have it, then you will see the best in life and the best in people. And by doing this, you will be a good example for all. You know, if you have a good attitude on life, then everyone you associate with will have a good attitude. Doesn't that sound good? If you think that your example is not as good as it should be, then that can be changed today because you are what you want to be. So you need to *want* to be a good example, and begin working toward that *today*.

Discipline

Let us begin with you young people first. I know most of the time

16

you don't think discipline is necessary. All I can say to that is just wait until you have children of your own. Then you will see the importance of discipline. For now, let me suggest a few things for your consideration. When your parents exert discipline, accept it, and never reject it. I know at times they may be wrong in their decision, but at the time they thought it was right, and in time when they see they were mistaken, they will make it up to you. If your parents didn't love you, then they would not discipline you at all. Here is what the Bible says about it in Proverbs 13:24: "He that spareth his rod hateth his son: but he that loveth him chasteneth him betimes." You see, when they discipline you, they are doing what God has said, and they want you to develop into a great person. They want the best for you.

Now those of us who are parents, if we love our children, then we will discipline them. I don't beat my boys. I probably haven't whipped them over twice in the last year. But they know that when I must discipline them, they are really going to get it. To discipline a child, you don't have to whip them all the time. As a matter of fact, some children may never need a whipping. You can take things away from them or not give them things they want. Try different things with them. Let me tell you something that bothers me about some parents. I know my boys are not angels, and we have to continually discipline them. But what gets me is when parents let their children talk back to them and let them get away with almost anything. This sounds bad, but I wish someone would slap the *parent* when this happens. The child doesn't need to be slapped; it is the parent who needs it for letting the child act that way. Parents, if you expect your children to become good citizens and faithful Christians, then you must discipline them. God has given them to you for only a short time, so you must make that time count every day.

Family

The best thing about children is that they make up a family. One thing that really stands out in the Bible is that when you read of a family, you read how the whole family served God. We read of a wealthy woman named Lydia who was baptized along with her household (Acts 16:11-15). This is a good example showing us that we need the whole family to serve God together. Can't you see all the advantages in this? You can pray together; you can go to worship together as a family. You will have the church in common. No one will be nagging the others to go to church. There are so many advantages that no one should ever lose this position of wealth. There is another good example in Acts 16:25-34. The jailor and his whole household were baptized into Christ for the remission of their sins. Isn't it great to see a family serve God together? When a family serves God together, it makes a big difference in a marriage and with children. It causes less arguing, less sadness, and less of everything that is evil. Oh, I don't mean to say that a Christian family doesn't have any problems. Sure, they do. But they also have God to help them with those problems. Do you?

If we expect our children to be faithful to God when they grow up, then before they are born, and while they are young, we need to be like Hannah of old. In 1 Samuel, she dedicated her son Samuel to God. She made sure that he put God first in his life. We must have the same dedication as old Hannah. The family that prays together, stays together.

Working Outside The Home

This has caused more problems with young people than anything else I can think of. It seems in today's world that as soon as our children turn 16, they get a job outside the home. We spend 15 years trying to get them to work *in* the home, and as soon as they turn 16 they want a job *outside* the home. There are a few children who turn 16 and need a job to help support their family. That's okay. A few want to work one or two days a week outside the home. That's okay! But, dear friends, when they turn 16 and we allow them to work outside the home when they don't need the money, we do them, ourselves, and the church great harm. Let me show you the harm it causes:

1. The home-life is upset
2. The church is neglected
3. They grow up too fast
4. School work is neglected

Home life Upset

As soon as they begin to work at 16, then our home life is upset. We are unable to have all the family together even at mealtime. We are unable to have a family Bible study because everyone is not there. And don't you think they need the Bible study more than they do the money which they receive at work? It will cause a lot of disagreement at home—from who will take them to work to what they will do with their money. Most young people at 16 are not mature enough to handle a job. Many go from job to job. They never find what they want in life and this is no way to build character. A peaceful home is much better than money. Don't you agree?

Church neglected

I have seen this many times in my life. How sad it is to place a dollar above the church. If your 16 year old is working, ask yourself and him this question: "Will this job cause you to miss a Wednesday night service, Sunday morning or Sunday night service, or any actively that the teens have at church - from teen devotions to teen fun and games?" If they miss any of these, then you, dear parent, must not let that 16 year old work outside the home. And you, 16 year old, must not take a job that will cause you to miss any of these services. Dear teen, without the church you don't have anything. If you do have to work, then please don't miss anything that relates to the church, okay? The choice is yours. Do you want a job which might cause you to be a weak Christian, or do you want to be as strong as you can in serving God?

Grow up too fast

Have you ever wondered why children today are dating at 13? What about young girls getting pregnant? In Tennessee alone, the number of girls between the ages of 10 and 13 who are becoming pregnant has doubled from 1984 to 1985. Have you thought about all the makeup they put on at ages 10-16? The makeup companies have. They are the number one seller to young people. What about so many accidents with young people who drive especially while drinking alcoholic beverages? Why do you think insurance companies have to charge so much for young people? Who drive? It is because within two months most 16 year olds will have an accident.

Now to answer all the above questions, and hundreds more like them. *WE LET THEM GROW UP TOO FAST!!!* We cannot blame everything on the young person. It's our fault. We let them and at times even encourage them to grow up too fast. I imagine I have told Todd a hundred times to grow up. We expect them to act like adults, but they are children, and we must not take that child-like attitude way from them. If they grow up too fast, then before long they will leave us, and we will wish that they were children again. I want my boys to stay home with us at least until they are 21, and even longer. I realize that it wasn't meant for them to stay with us forever, but please let them grow up on their own, and don't push them!

Now you young people, just because everyone else is doing something, that doesn't mean that you have to. I realize that peer pressure is a big problem, but if your friends do things - from driving, to working—and you don't want to, then tell them so, and let them go on without you.

School work neglected.

Once you begin a job at 16, your grades usually begin to drop at school. Most of your jobs will be at night when you should be studying for the next day. Also you will find yourself tired and even falling asleep during classes at school. You won't be able to spend any time with your friends at school, because you have to go on to work. It will be hard for you to participate in sports because you will have to be at work. And what about those Friday night football games? Your friends will be there, but you will at work. Dear young people, if you can keep from working outside the home at age 16, then do it. At this age you need school. You need friends, you need those ballgames, you need church activities, you need time with your parents. So please think about this before you go to work. I realize that you will have more things if you work outside the home, but who said that more is better?

Final Note:

I wish there were a definitive answer to raising children. I wish there were a definitive answer for you young people when you have to make a decision that is difficult. The only thing that I can tell the parent and the child is that I make mistakes with my boys, and so will you. But the best way for everything to work out for the best is to make sure that God is on your side. And the only way that God will be on your side is for you to be a Christian and to continually ask Him for His guidance and help. If you are not a Christian, then please read these scriptures. I pray that they may be of some help to you.

Mark 16:16; Luke 13:3; Romans 10:10; Matthew 28:18-20; Acts 2:38; Romans 6:3-5; Galatians 3:27.

Children

1. What do you think children are thinking about us?

2. How can children break your heart?

3. Discuss Ephesians 6:4.

4. Why is the church so important to our children?

5. Why should children watch who they choose as friends?

6. Who is our best example?

7. Why should we make our children obey us?

8. What do children lose by taking jobs outside the home at age 16?

9. Why is it important for our children not to grow up too fast?

10. Do we make mistakes with our children?

THE CHURCH

The Church

The church can be many things to many people. To me one thing that the church is, is a place where sinners like you and me help each other while we are serving God. The church is not the building in which we meet. The building is a *place*. The church is God's people. We refer to our attending church services, as "going to church." I guess that's okay, but it would be more scriptural to say "We are going to the church building." The church is made up of people who are Christians, (Christlike), who are trying to live a better life. It is not made up of sinless people, people who never do wrong. It is made up of people who realize that they are sinners and need forgiveness from God.

Many people say, "I would not go to that church because they are all hypocrites." I hope you don't think like that. Sure, we sometimes do things that are wrong. Sure, we sin. Sure, we could do better. But that is why we are in the church, so we can keep from sinning and continually try to do better. But dear friend, don't you think it is better being in the church, trying to serve God, than to be on the outside calling people hypocrites? The church is made up of all kinds of people. Some sin a lot, some a little, and probably some hardly sin at all, but all are trying to do better. Just because someone is a Christian doesn't mean that we are not tempted like everyone else. It only means that in the church we try to work on those temptations and to stay away from evil.

What Is The Church?

The word "church" is used by more people in this world than any other word. And still most folks don't understand the meaning of it. Let's notice some things about the church.

I hear people every day say "my church", "your church", "our church", "my parent's church", etc. Many treat this word as if it were just a common thing, such as a chair, or some other type of furniture. In the Bible it is very simple what the church is. But people still misunderstand it.

First, the church is not a material house, or a building as many seem to think. The church is a spiritual house. Peter says, (1 Peter 2:5): "Ye also, as lively stones, are built up a *spiritual house,* an holy priesthood, to offer up spiritual sacrifices, acceptable to God by Jesus Christ." The church is people who have been called out of the world to serve God. 2 Thessalonians 2:14 says: "Whereunto he called you by our gospel, to the obtaining of the glory of our Lord Jesus Christ." The church is made up of people who have been saved from their sins. Acts 2:47 says "Praising God, and having favour with all the people. And the Lord added to the church daily such as should be saved." Those who make up the body of Christ are His church. Ephesians 1:22,23 and Colossians 1:18. When we want to find out the right church we must be a part of, there are a few things that we should look for. Let us mention only a few. It is not enough just to be a part of some church, because Jesus built only one true church (Matthew 16:18). Therefore, He is only pleased with that one church. When you are looking for a church, look for the following:

A Church That Goes By The Bible Alone.

If you are a part of an organization that bases its belief upon something other than the Bible, then you are in the wrong church. The Bible is all we need and all that we can have as our guide. Because it thoroughly furnishes us with all things that we need to make it to heaven. And isn't that what we are trying to do? (2 Timothy 3:16,17). Since the word of God is perfect, that is all we need.

A Church That Uses The Whole New Testament
For Its Plan Of Salvation

It is so easy to use one verse of the Bible out of context and say that is all you need. Dear friend, we are not allowed to do that. If we only take part of the Bible, then we will end up in hell. No one wants that. How sad it is that many preachers and religious leaders won't teach the whole plan of salvation to lost souls. I don't always understand why. Here is what the Bible teaches about the plan of salvation. Please look up these scriptures for yourself.

1. *HEAR,* John 12:47.
2. *BELIEVE,* Mark 16:16; John 8:24.
3. *REPENT,* Mark 6:12; Acts 17:30; Luke 13:3,5.
4. *CONFESS,* Matthew 10:32; Romans 10:9; 1 John 1:9; 1 John 4:15.
5. *BE BAPTIZED,* Mark 16:16; Acts 2:38; Acts 2:41; Acts 8:12; Acts 8:38; Acts 9:18; Acts 10:48; Acts 16:15; Acts 16:33; Acts 18:8; Acts 19:3,5; Romans 6:3; Galatians 3:27; 1 Peter 3:21.

Now, dear friend, you have looked these scriptures up in your Bible. How can you be a part of any group that doesn't obey all five steps when it comes to the plan of salvation? Show these scriptures to your preacher, teacher, or anyone you may be studying with. Ask them why their church doesn't teach this. If they will be honest with you, they must admit that they are not teaching the whole council of God. So you need to look for a church that teaches all of God's word. You see, most churches, just obey three or four of these steps concerning salvation, but God wants you and me to obey all five of them. The choice is yours, who will you choose - man or God?

A Church That Partakes Of Communion Every Sunday (The First Day Of The Week)

The early church took communion to remember the death of Jesus every first day of the week, or Sunday. I won't say much on this. I'm going to let you come to the right conclusion with just two scriptures. Acts 20:7 and 1 Corinthians 16:1,2. Read these scriptures carefully. Notice one says the early church had communion on the first day of the week and the other says they had a collection (or giving) on the first day of the week. Ask yourself and your preacher this question: If the saints in the Bible had the collection on the first day of the week (Sunday), then isn't it correct that we must have it then also? He will agree with that because most likely every church has a collection every Sunday. Now the same words are found in Acts 20:7. They had the communion every first day of the week. Ask your preacher why your church doesn't have it also every first day of the week. If he can't give you a good answer (and he can't), if that church just accepts that and doesn't carry out the scriptural example, then, dear friend, you are in the wrong church. Look for one that goes by what the Bible says.

A Church That Uses No Instrument Of Music In Worship To God

I want you to use your mind on this one also. I want you to be honest and draw your own conclusion, and then do what is right. Notice Ephesians 5:19; Colossians 3:16; James 5:13; Revelation 15:3; Romans 15:9; 1 Corinthians 14:15; Matthew 26:30; Mark 14:26; Revelation 5:9; Revelation 14:3; Acts 16:25.

These are all the scriptures in the New Testament that pertain to music and singing in the New Testament Church. Notice that none of these scriptures imply use of an instrument of music while they were singing. We are commanded to sing and not to play. In the Old Testament, they used instruments of music, but we are not under the Old Testament today. We have a new law and we are under the New Testament. Dear friend, if your church uses an instrument of music in worship, then it has no scriptural authority for it. So why stay there? Go to one that doesn't use an instrument of music in worship. We are not here to please ourselves, but to please God. If we expect to make it to heaven, we must live only to please God. There are over 400 denominations in the world. The best advice that I can give you is to read your Bible and go to the church that goes by the Bible and nothing else!

The Church

1. What is the church?

2. What type of people make up the church?

3. How many churches did Jesus build?

4. Explain the plan of salvation.

5. Can we leave anyone of the five steps of salvation out?

6. Name the acts of worship.

7. Did the early church use instruments of music?

8. Discuss the importance of not adding to or taking away from God's word.

Communication

I believe that communication within the family is one of the most important things that we could ever have. I believe that most of our problems arise from lack of communication. Once a husband and wife fail to communicate, their marriage will surely fail. Communication is vital to a marriage in order for it to work. I also believe that once we quit communicating with our children, our family begins to fall apart. If you agree with me on most of what I have said, and you want to have better communictation with your loved ones, then I'm sure this chapter will help you as much as it has helped me. Let us now notice a few ideas that will help us to communicate better.

Making A Marriage Work

I know most people believe that marriage is give and take. I disagree with that. I believe that marriage is a give and give situation. To make a marriage work, we have to be willing to give and never take. There are many things that the husband can do that the wife cannot. On the other hand, there are many things that the wife can do that the husband cannot. So to make a marriage work, it takes both people trying their best, doing what they can do best, utilizing their best traits. Each partner needs to rely upon the strength of the other. There will be times when you must make a decision about things which you can't agree on. The answer to that is in 1 Peter 3:1. "Likewise, ye wives, be in subjection to your own husbands; that if any obey not the word, they also may without the word be won by the conversation of the wives."

The main point here is subjection. The Bible teaches us that the husband will be held accountable for the family, so he must have the final say. To communicate well then, the husband must be in charge. That is not to say the wife doesn't have any say, because a man would be very foolish if he thought he could make all the decisions and do everything without his wife. That is why God gave him a wife, to be a help-mate for him. She helps him to make decisions and to run the home more efficiently. The husband must be willing to listen to his wife's point of view, because many times the wife has a better head on her shoulders than her husband does. Many husbands, including me, have been saved from a lot of trouble and embarrassment because they took time to listen to what their wives had to say. I believe that we need to consult our wives before we make a lot of our decisions. And the same thing holds true for the wives. Before you go out and buy a lot of clothes, tell your husband first, and if he is wise, he will encourage you to do so. But when you do this without telling him, then look out! I learned a good lesson along this line many years ago. One day I came home with a new car that Ruby didn't know anything about. To make a long and painful story short, the day I sold that car was the day I got off the couch. Well, it actually wasn't to that extreme, but she was happy when *we* sold that car.

To communicate better and to make a marriage work better, then it must begin with yourself. It is so easy to criticize your mate because of the way she or he handles things. But to make it work better, we need to point that finger at ourselves first and last. If we are not willing to look in the mirror at our own faults, then how can we criticize our mates about their faults? And isn't that what Jesus taught in Matthew 7:1-5?

Lack Of Communication Causes Divorce

Isn't it sad that just because something so simple as communication in a marriage fails, divorce comes as a result? I was talking to a young girl the other day. She told me she was going to get a divorce because her husband hit her. He had never hit her before, and he had always been good to her. They had only been married for about four months. I believe she forgot her vows "for better or for worse." However, I believe that a man is a coward if he hits a woman. I certainly would not condone that. But I believe the real problem is communication.

Its so easy to get a divorce, much easier than to talk our problems out. To make a marriage work, we must be determined to *work* on it. Nothing is free anymore, we must *work* in order to have a good marriage. Some men think that in order to get their wives' attention, they have to hit them over the head. Try to turn that situation around. What if you would not listen to your wife, and she laid you out with a frying pan. Would you listen to her then? Not me. I would want to get away from that person. I would not want to communicate with her. If you expect your wife to listen to you, then give her flowers, candy, or a kiss and a smile, and then talk to her. If I want a positive answer from Ruby about something, I try to get her in a good mood first. I believe she does me the same way, too. As an old saying goes, "you can catch more flies with sugar than with salt." When I first began preaching, I thought if I were going to get people to do what was right everytime I preached, I had to tell them that they were going to hell if they didn't do what God demands of them. I believe that I get more positive response today because of my attitude and how I relate to people. Now this same pattern will work with the husband and wife. Treat one another in a kind way and you will be able to work out any problem that you will ever have.

Be Understanding

Its a sad day when a husband or wife won't listen to what the mate has to say about a certain subject. I have been in homes where the husband is so overbearing that he won't let his wife say anything. I have also been in homes where the wife is the same way. To be a good husband or wife, and to communicate well, we must be understanding enough to stop and listen to our partner. I believe if we would do that, it would surprise us how intelligent and how much our mate really knows. Most of the best ideas I have ever gotten were from someone else. You see, if we will take time to understand what someone is trying to say, we will learn a lot more from them. Ruby is very quiet and doesn't have much to say, but when she speaks, I listen, because I realize that wisdom comes from her lips.

Have you ever noticed when you say something or do something, the reaction you get from your mate? That is feelings coming out. When that happens, don't ignore it. Stop and ask why he or she acted that way. If you don't, then you might continue to say or do things your mate does not approve of. Many arguments could have been avoided if someone would have only stopped and considered the feelings of the mate. Everyone has their point of view about certain things, and if your mate objects to your view, then you need to talk it over and try to work things out. If you ignore problems, they have a way of getting bigger and bigger as time goes by.

I have noticed over the years how some people, after they stop talking, also stop listening. I don't fully understand why people can't listen to someone else. Many times when someone else is talking, we are thinking of something else to say to them. Beloved, to communicate well, and especially with our mates, then we must listen to what they say before we begin to think what our answer will be about a certain subject. There are too many hard-headed people in this world, who won't listen to anyone. Let us make sure that we will not be like one of them. I have caught myself many times when I'm in a meeting, first thinking about my own ideas that I want to bring up when it is my turn to speak. That's wrong. Because everyone has ideas and they deserve our undivided attention. We can bring our ideas up in due time, but until it is our time, we need to listen to others ideas. If we are afraid that we might forget them, then we need to write them down and forget about them until our time comes to speak. I have noticed that if we just wait and listen, before long someone else had the same idea that I had and most of the time they have a better way of making it work out. When this happens, you can be 100 percent behind their idea, and help them work on it. Some of the happiest days of my married life are when Ruby thinks of something that I have been thinking about for a long period of time. When this happens, we can work together on it and enjoy that idea more than if it were my idea alone.

Watch What You Communicate

I am sure that you have seen people who make a habit of saying whatever is on the tip of their tongues. I have been guilty of this a lot of times and I'm sure you have, too. If there is anything in communication that we need to work on, that's it. Someone said, "Make sure that your mind is in gear before your tongue takes off." I believe we need to live by that statement. We must realize that once we say something, then it is gone from our control. Sure, you can say, "I'm sorry", but once you hurt someone with your tongue, most of the time that person will never forget it. He will probably forgive you, but the memory cannot be erased. It has been said that a tongue three inches long can kill a man six feet tall. Is it any wonder that the Bible says these words in Proverbs 18:21, "Death and life are the power of the tongue: and they that love it shall eat the fruit thereof."

I like the words of James, in chapter 2. Read the whole chapter and it will help you to understand a little more about how serious the words we speak are. James says the words we speak can control our whole life. If we expect to communicate well with our mate, we need to choose our words well. One wrong word can control the whole day, or even longer. Notice when something is said wrong, how the whole day will have many things go wrong in it. I like to start the day with a smile or a song. If you start a day this way, then your day will go a lot better. We have a rule at our house that no one leaves home angry or upset. Many times when the boys don't get what they want before school or work, we have to try to change the atmosphere before they leave. This is very hard to do, but if we, or our children, kick the cat before we leave home, then we will kick something all day. When we come home, the old cat better not be in our way!

I like to kiss Ruby and say kind words to her before I go to work. I like for the boys to see me do that, too. I believe this helps Ruby, myself, and the boys. If we can only leave home in the mornings with kind words and a positive attitude, then I believe that we can overcome any obstacle that may get in our way that day.

Be Ye Angry And Sin Not

I am so glad that Ephesians 4:26 is in the Bible. That scripture understands human nature. In life, there are times that we disagree with our mates and with other people. To communicate well, we need to understand that we have a right to get angry, but we don't have a right to take it out on someone else, and we certainly cannot sin through our anger. Can you imagine going through life agreeing with everything your mate says and does? As long as two people live together, they are going to disagree on a few things. When we are angry with our mate, or with someone else, then the best thing for us to do is to sit down together and talk it out. I believe that a lot of marriage problems would be solved if we would take the time and talk to each other. There are many things on our mind that we need to let our mate know about. Consider the example of your wife wearing an outfit that you don't really care much for. I'll bet if you had told her that before she bought it, she would not have purchased it. I believe that our mates buy most of their clothing to please us, so we owe each other the courtesy and respect to tell them what we think about things. By the way, make sure you tell them in a kind way, because no one should deliberately hurt another person's feelings.

There are times that we get angry with our mates because something they have done (or not done). When a husband leaves his clothes all over the house, instead of getting upset and arguing with him, take time to tell him how much that bothers you. If he is a considerate husband, he won't do anything that will get you upset and angry. The same things holds true for the wife.

Don't Let The Sun Go Down Upon Your Wrath (Ephesians 4:26)

Ruby and I have a promise to each other, and that is we never go to sleep at night if we are angry with each other. To communicate well and to save a lot of restless nights, I highly recommend this to everyone. There is no room in a marriage for two people to go to bed angry and wake up angry. Usually if you wake up angry, then the whole day is going to be a bad one for you. If you want to start the day off right, then by all means don't leave the house angry, and by all means never slam the door behind you. I must confess that I have done that before, and I felt bad the whole day. I pray to God that will never happen to me again. I hope that will be your prayer, also.

If we expect our children to grow up in a way that we want them to, then we had better not go to bed arguing and fighting. If we conduct ourselves this way, then there is a good chance that they will act the same way once they have a family of their own. We might think that we are fooling them, but believe me, they know more about us than we think.

Communication

1. Concerning unchangeable disagreements, explain 1 Peter 3:1.

2. To have better communication, where is a good place to begin?

3. Will a lack of communication cause a divorce? Explain.

4. Do you listen to what your mate, children, parents have to say?

5. Why is it important to listen to someone else's ideas?

6. Why should we watch and not say the first thing that comes to our mind?

7. Explain why it is important to start the day out by being happy?

8. Why is it important to let our mate know what is on our mind?

9. Discuss Ephesians 4:26.

HOSPITALITY

Hospitality

O ne of the most important things that a family needs today is hospitality. Have you ever wondered why this country is losing hospitality? I have. I know part of the reason for it. We are a generation of people who are too busy. We spend more time on the road and at work then we do at home. The home has become like a filling station. We come in, get filled up and head out again. This is the main reason why I am writing this book — to help us improve on our home life. To prove to you that we are a country that is losing hospitality, let me ask you a few questions:

1. Do you know your neighbors' names within two or three houses of your house?
2. Have you had your next door neighbors into your home?
3. Have you had your next door neighbors in your home for a meal?
4. Do you visit your neighbors?
5. Do you have social activities with your neighbors?

You probably only answered yes to three or four of the questions, or maybe even less. I can only answer yes to *one* of the questions, so you see I need this chapter as much as you do. I don't have all the answers and God, (and a lot of other people) know that I am not perfect. But I'll bet by the time I'm through writing this book, I will improve on my hospitality. Won't you make the same commitment today? Let us notice a few topics on hospitality. If you think of anything else, then write them in this book; makes notes that will help you.

What Is Hospitality?

Hospitality can be just about any act of kindness. It can range from a meal to a smile. I like both of them. There are many ways to be hospitable to people. I like to have a meal with people as our form of hospitality. Let me give you some suggestions on hospitality. Start at church, and invite members of the church over to your home. This will help them to get to know you better and you will learn more about them at the same time. Plan on inviting them over, set aside a day and it wil all work out. But if you don't plan on doing it, then you may never have them into your home. Ruby and I plan on having an annual picnic at our home every August. We have about 200 to 250 people from the church every year and we all have a great time. Everyone looks forward to it each year. We have about 50 people from church every New Year's Eve. This is a great time. We have our annual chili dinner every winter with 50 or 60 people from church. We have the teenagers from church over for a devotional two or three times a year. I'm sure you can see by now that the church is our life. I hope it is yours, too. I believe that we need to do more things with the church now than ever before.

Hospitality can be taking people places. For instances, taking an older person to the store, or to the bank, etc. Hospitality is being friendly to people, trying to smile a lot and show your hospitality. Someone has said that a dog is loved by the old and the young, because it wags its tail and not its tongue. Show your smile and people will see how friendly you are. When someone visits you, make them feel like Kings and Queens. Make them feel at home. Try your best to get them to stay and come back again. To be hospitable you must be pleasant to people, show them that you care for them and are interested in them and their lives.

One reason why we should use hospitality is because we will be judged by it one day. Read Matthew 25. Jesus speaks about giving people something to eat, drink and about helping the sick and those in prison. You see, hospitality involves helping people, and that's something that all of us can and must do. We have no excuse not to show hospitality. Jesus won't accept any excuse, so why should we even make up one?

Hospitality could be described as *giving of yourself.* Notice you don't need money or fame to give of yourself. Everyone can give of oneself to others. When we help others (and that's what hospitality is all about), then it is as if we are helping Jesus. For Jesus said in Matthew 25:40, "I tell you the truth, whatever you did for one of the least of these brothers of mine, you did it for me." Paul tells Timothy that it is a requirement for an elder of the church to have hospitality, 1 Timothy 3:2. So you see how important it is to God.

Hospitality must always be shown to the poor. About five years ago Ruby met an old retired school teacher named Miss West. She has no family and lives in a local nursing home. Every year we have her over for Thanksgiving dinner. We look forward to it every year. We hope she lives many more Thanksgivings. We need to help people like this who can't return the deed. This world thrives on "I'll help you, if you'll help me." I'm not going to be that way, are you? The poor will always be with us, so show them hospitality now. You know when you help these people they feel good, but I believe we feel better than they do. That's why Jesus said it is more blessed to give than to receive.

Begin Hospitality Today

Today would be a good time for you to start planning on using hospitality. Start at church, work, with friends, at school, etc. Make a list of people whom you would like to get to know better. After you have that list, then begin thinking of ways to be hospitable to them. A good way to use hospitality is to look for a new person in the community. When they move in, be the first one there and see if you can be of some assistance. Offer your services, make a cake or help them arrange their furniture. I am sure there are a lot of good ideas that you can come up with when someone moves into your community. So start now thinking of ways that you can be hospitable to them.

Another good way to meet new people and to show them hospitality is to look for new people who visit where you worship. They are looking for a home, a place to worship God. Be the first one to have them into your home. Ruby and I make it a practice to have these people over the first time we see them. Sunday night after church works out well for us. Maybe it would be good for you, also. They usually only stay one or two hours, and it doesn't take much time for it. We always invite another family or two along with them, so we can have more people to enjoy the fellowship. We just have sandwiches or something light. Our main reason is not to eat, but to visit and try to get to know the people who visit church that Sunday. Many good things will come from this type of hospitality. You will get to know people better. You will care more for them the next time you see them. Most of the time they will find a home with the church there, and all this might have happened just because you used hospitality. Can you see how important hospitality is? Many great things have happened just because of hospitality. I wish I could express to you the joy that Ruby and I have received from having people into our home. And especially those who are new in the church. We love to visit with them and show them that they have a friend whom they can call upon.

I think that many of us don't use hospitality because we expect too much. We think everything has to be perfect before we can have anyone into our home. We think the house has to be spotless first (we *live* in our home and we don't expect a spotless house and neither should you). We think we are too busy to have someone over. That's no excuse, because everyone has 24 hours in a day. So we do what we want to do. Some people are nervous when they have someone over. But after the people have left, you then feel good and realize that it wasn't so bad after all. I believe the more you have people over, the more you will enjoy it and the less nervous you will be. Another excuse is that their house is better than ours, or something like that. We have friends who are doctors, lawyers, own their own businesses, and they come to our home and feel welcome. It doesnt matter what you have or what you don't have. Just be yourself and everything will work out.

There are many things that can be said about hospitality. The best thing I can tell you about it is to begin *today* using it!

Hospitality

1. Is hospitality really important?

2. Why is there a falling away of hospitality?

3. What *is* hospitality?

4. Explain Matthew 25 in terms of hospitality?

5. Explain the importance of planning hospitality events.

6. Why are people nervous about having people into their homes?

Television

As far as preaching the Gospel and converting lost souls to Jesus, television is a good thing. There are also some good educational shows on for children. But overall, T.V. is the worst thing that a family could have in their home. All of us are guilty of watching this idiot box. Before you think I am a fanatic against T.V., let us look at a few things, okay? I will mention a few and we will talk about them in order.

1. Television has filth on it.
2. Television takes away from family time.
3. Television creates a bad attitude.
4. Satellites increase all the bad things that are already there.

Filth On T.V.

There are a lot of programs that have cursing, taking God's name in vain, using sex to attract viewers, etc. Violence is so bad that little children are shooting people with their finger and expecting them to die. The violence and sex that we and our children watch will come out in action one day. In 1972, after a two year study, the Surgeon General of the U.S. found that television violence *does* affect our behavior. The new cable channels and satellites that are bringing filth into the homes every day are a disgrace to the home. God is not pleased when we watch things like this. I know you know what programs I am talking about, and maybe your children even watch them. May God spare our lives long enough to repent and get this filth out of our homes. When filth comes on, don't let your conscience be seared with a hot iron (1 Timothy 4:2). Get up and change the channel or turn it off, please!

Takes Away From The Family

When the television is on, the family is off. The average American child spends 15,000 hours watching television before he graduates from High School. Every hour that is spent watching T.V. is an hour that is robbing our family of becoming closer together and closer to God. I have noticed my boys, as soon as a commercial comes on, begin to argue and fight. I wonder where they get that. Television, no doubt. I also notice when we are watching a religious program and a commercial comes on they don't argue and fight. Some programs can be good. Most are bad. Have you noticed traits like this in your children? If not, then try that experiment and do something about it. The answer is less of the world (TV.) and more of God. Time spent in front of the television is time spent away from school work and studying the Bible. In a sense, I guess that we are what we watch. How long would it take us watching bad things on T.V. before we begin to think bad and do bad things? I don't know, but I don't think it would take too long, do you? We as Christians have so many things in this world pulling the family apart. It seems like the family is going its separate ways. We don't eat together, play together, or sleep together anymore. So when we are together (and that should be more often), let's make it the best time of our life. The best way to do that is to turn the television off and spend that precious time together as a family.

Creates A Bad Attitude

Have you ever noticed how people react to things and actions of people? Try an experiment some time. Walk by people in a mall or grocery store and smile and say hello to them, or just smile and nod as you pass by. They will smile back at you. Try another experiment. When talking in a group, say something nice about someone in that group (and *mean* it). Before long they will say something good about you. Try one more thing. When you see someone you know, say something good about their dress or suit, (be honest), or something they have on. Then they will return it by saying your clothes look good, also.

I said all that in a positive attitude just to show you how the T.V. gives us a bad attitude. Had I said the opposite of the above, then it would have all been in a negative attitude. One example is to tell someone they look sick. They will tell you (or at least think it), that you don't look so good yourself. Now let's see what the T.V. does to our attitude.

On T.V. when kids see cartoons in which fighting and killing people are taking place with a certain type of gun, then when they see that gun in a store, what do they want? And why do they want it? Of course, they want the gun to play like they are killing people.

Now what about the teenage children, when they watch the "Dukes of Hazzard" as they fly through the air, or jump over a barn with their car. You guessed it. When they get into dad's car, they can imagine, and even try to see how fast they can go. Sometimes on two wheels. The bad part about this is that on television you can witness horrible wrecks in which the people involved get out and walk away. That is not how it is in real life! It is easy to see how a bad example can lead people astray. Those speeding cars are not as bad as all the violence and sex that you can see on television, but they have a definite negative influence.

Now what about us adults? Yes, it gives us a bad attitude, also. When you are watching a program where someone has a huge, fancy house, cars, money, etc., then before long we will be wanting the things that they have and maybe even getting them the way the television characters do - by cheating, stealing, etc. I also believe a lot of marriages are destroyed through T.V. Many men and women watch programs where the husband or wife looks better and treats their mate better in the T.V. show, than their mate treats them in real life. Dear friends, most of those people on T.V. have a terrible home life, and yours is so much better than theirs. They would give anything to be in your shoes. The main advice that I could give you is to be happy and content with what you have, because the grass isn't greener on the other side of the fence. The fish aren't biting on the other side of the lake. The family isn't any better off on the other side of town than your family is. Just thank God and be happy that you even have a family.

Satellites

Isn't it strange how some things can bring forth good and bad? This sounds like James 3:10: "Out of the same mouth proceedth blessing and cursing. Now that the satellite system has become economically reasonable to the normal person, you can see them everywhere. They bring some good entertainment into the home. Through this system, the gospel is preached all over the world. As far as the good things it does, I am all for it. But the bad things that are on it, I am completely against. Right now they have a playboy channel, where nothing but sex is on. Who knows what will be next?

Because of programs like this, it turns me against the satellite. I can't stand people who tell me and others that all you have to do is turn it off. I believe the best way is not to have it in your home in the first place. Let me give you a personal example. I would not watch the playboy channel for anything. But probably if I had a satellite in my home, I would be greatly tempted to turn to that channel. I believe you would face the same temptation. Our curiosity would get the better of us, and we would watch it. So why flirt with temptation? Don't even have one in your home. It seems like at times we try to see how close we can get to temptation, without falling. What we should do is to try and see how far away we can get from it. There are so many temptations in this world that bring us down in this life. When we see that something will hurt us as Christians, then we need to stay away from it. You know as well as I do that if we had one, then we would spend more time watching television than studying the Bible, going to worship, having Christian fellowship, doing personal evangelism, etc. We would spend more time watching television than with all these other things combined.

Dear friend, these things are important for us to make it to heaven. So none of us can waste our time watching television. If you have a satellite, and say that you don't watch the filth on it (which I doubt), then what about your children and grandchildren? You know they will turn it on, and you cannot be there every moment to keep them from it. So please keep them away from this temptation. Once you put filth into a child's mind, how can you get it out?

Note: T.V. And Marriage

I suggest that the newlyweds wait one year before they purchase a television. (Most won't wait one day.) You need that time together and the television will take it away from you. And I would highly suggest that no family ever have a television in their bedroom. This is a private place and should not be shared with Johnny Carson, or anyone but your mate.

Television

1. Can the television be good if it is used properly?

2. Will the violence on television affect our behavior?

3. Does the television take time away from the family?

4. Describe the effect the T.V. has on children, teens, and adults.

5. Explain James 3:10, and how it relates to television.

6. *Be honest!* Would you be tempted to watch a dirty movie on television if you thought no one knew you were watching it?

7. Discuss newlyweds, concerning television.

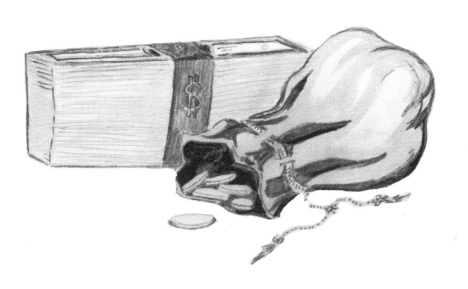

MONEY/MATERIALISM

Money And Materialism

I believe that God wants the best for His children. I think that is why He said in Matthew 6:33, "But seek ye first the kingdom of God and his rightcousness, and all these things shall be added unto you." God is saying that if we put Him first, then He will take care of us. I believe that, don't you? I guess the main problem with materialism is that we want more than what God wants us to have at that time. Maybe if we could wait on God, then we would receive things in due time. It is so easy to fall in love with the world. That is why the Bible warns us in 1 John 2:15 to love not the world.

Financial Problems

The main cause of financial problems is that we fail to understand 1 Timothy 6:7. It says that we brought nothing into this world and we will carry nothing out. We want to buy so many things, thinking (I guess) that we will take it all with us when we leave this life. Most young couples find themselves in debt even before the honeymoon. They expect to have everything that their parents worked 20 years to have. They forget, or didn't even know, the hard times their parents had to go through in order to get where they are now. I read once that young couples should buy nothing on credit except a house or car. I agree with that. I would strongly suggest that a young couple should buy an older house the first year of their marriage. This may sound strange to you, but let me explain why I make that statement. I am an investor in real estate. I have close to a million dollars worth of property. I know the importance in it, so let me give you some advice for free that would cost someone else around a thousand dollars, if it were given by a financial adviser.

If you want a house of your own, look in the paper for a house that is for sale by the owner. Find an ad that reads something like this:

> House for sale by owner.
> Owner financing, with
> low down payment.

This house can be bought without using any of your money (which you don't have much of at first). Ask the owner to finance the house for 15 to 20 years at a certain percentage. He is willing to do this and has already indicated that by the ad he had in the paper. Next he wants a low down payment, probably one to five thousand dollars. This would be no problem. First, ask him if he would also finance the down payment for six months. This way, you will be making two payments to the owner. Banks are very important, and I use them a lot, but if you can deal directly with the owner you will save money and time. If the owner refuses to finance the down payment, then borrow that one to five thousand from the bank, or save it up yourself within six months and use your savings for the down payment. If you expect to get rich through a savings account, then you will go broke trying it because inflation will grow faster than your savings.

Okay, you now have a house without using any of your money, or at least only a small part of it. You will have many repair bills, but expect that. Begin fixing the house up because you now have a home of your own. Fresh paint and shrubs will help you to double your money when you sell it. While putting money and time into your home, it will help you in two major ways.

The first way is that you won't have a lot of money to spend on things that you don't need in life. You will want to buy the things you need instead. This is one of the most important lessons in life.

The second way is that it will help the two of you to be as one. You won't have time to do a lot of things with the boys or girls. You can spend your time working and playing while improving your home.

This will keep you from paying house rent. You can use your money that ordinarily would go to rent and put it into your own home. There is nothing wrong with paying rent, just try to buy as soon as you can. To keep from having financial problems, try to pay cash for everything else (T.V., furniture, toys, etc.). It will surprise you how many things you can do without while waiting on the money to buy something. Credit can be a good thing if it is used correctly. I have never owned a credit card in my life, and I don't expect to ever have one. I have seen times while traveling that I could use one, but I still made it okay, with the help of God. Credit cards will let you buy things that you don't need too easily, so try to stay away from them. Once you have gained things of this world, don't forget what Solomon said. (Read,

Ecclesiastes chapter 2). We can learn from him, for he had it all and said it never brought him contentment. We need to be content with what we have. (Philippians 4:11; 1 Timothy 6:8; Hebrews 13:5). Please read these scriptures. Paul said that he has learned in whatever condition he was in to be content. I have learned that the more I gain in this life, the less I have. I believe that the simple way of life is worth more than we can ever know. It's so easy for us to look at the Amish, Quakers, Mennonites, etc., and say "I'm glad that I don't have it as hard as they do." I would not want to be like them either, but I would give all I have to know their contentment in life and their attitude toward worldly things. Dear friend, anyone can make money. Anyone can have "things". But only a few can be content with what they have. Won't you be one of that few?

The best lesson to learn with money and material things is to try to learn to live within your means. In other words, don't spend more than what you make. If you do, then sooner or later you will end up in trouble. Make sure you can pay for something before you buy it on the installment plan.

Attitude

All through this book you will read about attitude. The reason for this is that I believe everything we do, and everything that relates to us, rests on our attitude. Our attitude can be the best thing, or the worst thing about us. It can make us or break us. It can make friends or enemies. It can give us a raise at work or a cut in our pay. It will determine whether we move on in life and succeed, or stay still and fail. I hope that your attitude will begin to improve right now. I can see you smiling. You sure are going to make it! Let me suggest some things about a proper attitude that will help you in money and material matters. First, let's say you want a raise at work. Look at your job and see ways that you can improve on your performance; then work on it. Tell your boss some of those ideas. I don't mean to brown-nose. I mean to be positive at work and things will work out a lot better. I believe that many of us lose our positive attitude the longer we work at a job. The best way to change that is to remember how you first wanted that job. Then remember how many people would like to have your job. After you done that, then be thankful that you have your position. I believe that this will give you a better attitude, and in return it will cause you to make more money, or at least it will help you to appreciate your paycheck.

Now let's look at another money saver. Let's say you want to buy something, from a hat to a house. You might say, "What does an attitude have to do with this?" Well, my friend, it has everything in the world to do with it. I have saved from $10 to $10,000 just because of a positive attitude. Suppose you find a hat that you really like, but it is not exactly the color you want. Smile, and tell the salesperson that it is not the color you want. Tell them how nice they are to you (if they *are*. I don't give my business to a lot of people who are not nice to me.) Most likely they will reduce it $10 or so just because you are nice to them. This attitude will work on a lot of things. I have some rental properties that I have a real estate company manage for me. They usually charge ten percent of the rent for their services. With a positive attitude, plus being friendly to them, they manage the property - with me doing a lot of the work - for three percent. I save about $10,000 within 5 years. Now do you see how important an attitude is to me? I hope it is to you, also. I have had salesmen want to give up some or even all of their commission for a sale, just because of the way I treated them. Of course, I expect them to make money, and I don't take advantage of anyone. I believe the more people you help in life, the more people will help you. I love to help people. I love to see them smile and be happy.

Something That Money Cannot Buy

It is so sad to see broken homes today. When we see them, we all say, "I wonder what caused that family to break up?" I don't know a lot of answers to those questions, but I do know one thing. *Money cannot buy a happy home.* Money can buy just about anything, but never, never think that you can make a happy home with it. Most broken homes are caused by money and the material value which we place on things that will soon be gone. I believe that my family and I enjoy material things just as much as anyone else does. But to save a home, and possibly a soul, from hell we need to make sure that our money serves us and we don't serve it. If you want to have a happy home, and want to succeed in life, then do this. In all the money you have or ever will have, give the Lord His part. God gave it to us and we must give it back to Him. Look at 2 Corinthians 8:3: "For to their power, I bear record, yea, and beyond their power they were willing of themselves." This tells us that the churches in Macedonia were willing to give of their means. I think this is a good example for us to follow, don't you? You know, I have found out over the years that the more we give, the more we receive. It is sad that I didn't understand 2 Corinthians 9:6 years ago. Here is what is says: "He that soweth sparingly shall reap also sparingly, and he that soweth bountifully shall reap bountifully." Now that we know this, we have no excuse. We hold our family together with God's help.

Money And Materialism

1. Explain Matthew 6:33.

2. What is the main cause of financial problems?

3. Why do young married people want so much when they are first married?

4. Why are credit cards dangerous?

5. What is true contentment in life?

6. Discuss spending more than we make.

7. Why is the right type of attitude so important?

8. Name something that money cannot buy.

FRIENDS

Friends

O ne of the best things that we have in life are friends. We will never get to a point where we don't need any more friends. When I think of all the friends that I have, I smile, because I know they are part of the best things of my life. A friend is someone who will stay with you, no matter what problems you may have. I would like for us to notice a few things that relate to friends:

1. Best Friends
2. Church Friends
3. Friends at Work
4. Showing Yourself to be Friendly

Best Friends

Everyone should have a best friend. It is a shame that many of us don't have one. We will only have a few "best" friends in our lifetime. If you are married, then your best friend should be your husband or wife. The reason why I say this is because your mate should be the one you rely upon when you need to talk to someone, or when you need to be comforted. When you need advice, they will be the first one to help you. There are many reasons why your mate should be your best friend.

Now, if you are married and your mate is your best friend, then that is great, so let's go on. You also need another "best" friend who isn't your mate, because there may be times when you need to talk to someone *about* your mate. And if you don't have another best friend, then you just can't tell anyone about certain things, unless you have someone you can really trust. Now with your mate being your best friend, you will have something special that you will never find with any other best friend. So don't expect as great a relationship with anyone else. A best friend is someone who can help you take your mind off a lot of problems in this world. It seems as though we sometimes let a lot of problems get to us and we need someone to help us solve those problems. So there is where a best friend can really help. Listen to Solomon in Proverbs 18:24: "A man that hath friends must show himself friendly: and there is a friend that sticketh closer than a brother."

In order for us to have friends, we must be friendly. But here Solomon says that a friend stays with you, closer than a brother. That is a good feeling to know that you have a best friend who will always be close by. If you don't have a best friend, then look around and find one. You might meet a lot of good friends, so keep looking and before long you will find your best friend. They are out there, but you have to look for them. Also, to have a best friend requires time. It is not something you obtain overnight.

Church Friends

These friends will help you to have the best time of your life. I could not be a happy and positive person without my church friends. Ruby and I love having them in our home. We love being in their homes, too. We also love going places with them. I love my church friends more than any others that I have. It is so good to go places and do things with people who don't smoke, don't drink, and don't curse. Oh, I don't mean to say that we are perfect—far from that. But it is so good to laugh and have a good time with people who don't have these vices. I teach a Bible Class on the family, and I can hardly wait until Sunday comes, so I can be with my church friends in this Bible class. We have such a good time together, and it is exciting for all of us. If you are not a Christian, or if you want to see some good church friends together, especially in a Bible class, then let me personally invite you to our class. It is at the East Side Church of Christ in Cleveland, Tennessee. Come by and visit this class. I will be the one with the smile on his face, so look for me. Also, it will be hard to pick me out, because all of us are smiling, because we love each other so much. If you don't have what we have, then you are missing out on a lot of good fellowship with church friends. We are all sinners who are trying to do better and want to make it to heaven.

The best thing about our church friends is that there is no class distinction with us. There is neither black nor white, rich or poor, educated or uneducated, good or bad, we are all one in Christ. We realize that we sin and need help from God and each other. The world doesn't give you friends like this.

Friends At Work

This is the proving ground of your Christian life. This will be the hardest place for a Christian to live a Christian life. Most religious leaders don't understand what a Christian has to go through with at work. They are sheltered from the world and don't have this temptation of sin. At work, a Christian will be tempted, too. There is temptation to lie, steal, curse, cheat on their mate, drink, smoke, plus 10,000 other temptations. We all have to work at some type of job, so no matter where it is, we all need a friend at work. There are many advantages of having friends at work. Let me mention a few things that will help us at work, with friends and others:

1. Always have a positive attitude.
2. Always try to develop friendship at work.
3. Don't ge angry and upset with your co-workers.
4. Try to convert friends without pushing or nagging them.
5. Be a good example in everything you do.

Positive Attitude

At work, a smile and a positive attitude will get you the best job, the most pay, and more contentment with your job than any other person at work. No one, and I repeat *no one,* likes a person who has a negative attitude in life. Only the positive person will be able to tell others of a better life to live. Only the positive person will have true friends. If you are grouchy at work, then no one will want to be around you, much less listen to what you have to say. Try an experiment with people at work. Go for a month smiling and being friendly to people, and I'm sure you will like them better and they will like being around you more. Try it and I am sure you will like it. You will see the good in people and be able to overlook their faults. And we all have faults, we just need to overlook them in people and talk about their good points.

Friendship At Work

We all can use one more friend. I like friends and I like gaining new ones. A friend is something that we can never have too many of. At work you will find people who have all kinds of problems. The best way we can help them is to be a friend to them. Many people are like you; they are looking for a new friend. I have found out that even a person whom I thought would never be a friend to anyone, ends up being your best friend. We judge people too much by how they look and act, until we see what is on the inside. Work becomes much more pleasant when people around you become your friends. When you cannot get along with someone at work, then work becomes a problem in life. Work should not be a problem. It is something we all have to do. We all have problems at work from time to time, but we should enjoy our jobs, because our friends are there. Ruby and I have over 60 people working for us whom we can truthfully say are our friends, and we enjoy working with them. We really believe that we have the best people working for us, and we appreciate them. We know without God and them, we would not have what we have today. So to us (and I hope to you), friendship at work is very important.

Don't Get Angry And Upset At Work

It is hard to teach anyone when you or they are upset. At times all of us get angry and upset with people, because no one is as perfect as we are (just kidding). The best way to handle it is to back down and think about what you are saying before you say something that you will be sorry for later on. The Bible realizes that we get angry; it just tells us to control our anger. Ephesians 4:26 says; "Be ye angry and sin not."

The people whom we see and who see us at work are the ones whom we must be a good example to. These are the people who we are around more than any. If we expect to teach them, then we cannot get angry and display our tempers at work.

Be Friendly

It is always good to see someone with a smile on his face. A friendly person is always like and admired by others. Have you ever noticed how someone is always smiling, or has a positive outlook on life? We can have that same smile and that same positive attitude. Those people might have less than we have financially. They might have more problems than we do. They might even be treated badly. But one thing for sure is they don't let things get them down. The reason why I say that we can be friendly is because it is all in our minds. If we practice smiling, and try to improve on our attitude, then before long people will be looking at us and saying "I wish I could be that friendly!" Don't you know that a smile is contagious? You've probably heard the expression, "If you meet someone who doesn't have a smile, give him one of yours." Try it, you'll get one in return!

Friends

1. Why should we have a "best friend?"

2. Discuss Proverbs 18:24.

3. Why are church friends so important?

4. What would be the best thing you could do for your friends at work?

5. Give some examples of being friendly.

54

GOALS

Goals

A family without goals is like a sailboat without a sail. I believe we all need to have goals in life. There are many types of goals. Not everyone wants to have goals in life. I know many people who have a great family life and don't have any goals at all. I believe so strongly in goals because I don't think I could have accomplished what I have without them. I read a book in 1979 entitled "A Lazy Man's Way To Become A Millionaire." The book was all about setting goals and how to work to achieve them. That book did more for me personally (other than the Bible) than any other book has ever done. Let me share some ideas with you that I have learned over the past few years concerning goal setting.

There are so many goals in life that we can set, that we could never even dream of the number. Some are spiritual, physical, educational, social, work-related, play, eating, money, sleeping, etc. You name it and you can set a goal for it.

Spiritually

My first goal in life, and your should be the same, is spirituality. This needs to be a goal because it is not easy to be strong spiritually. There are so many things, and so many people in the world, who don't want us to be a spiritual giant. I have seen so many people become Christians and not become active in the church. I know why some of this is, it's because they are not trying to grow as a Christian. They don't set goals to be at all the services of the church. They don't see a goal to make new friends in their congregation. They don't set a goal to bring other friends to church. You see where I'm going. It takes goals to be spiritual. Why do you think some people know more Bible than others? It's because they set goals to read every day or night (2 Timothy 2:15, "Study to show thyself approved unto God a workman. . . .") Dear friend, I pray that you will set a goal today to be a better, more spiritual person. It doesn't matter how old you are, or how long you have been a Christian. You still can grow spiritually. A family that prays together, stays together. If your family is not all going to church together, then won't you set a goal today to begin attending together? I cannot imagine living a Christian life without Ruby to help me. If you are not going to worship, and your mate is, then lay this book down right now, and go tell your mate that you are going to start attending worship services with them. Watch how they smile, and expect a big hug and a few tears, for they have been praying for this day to come. Are you back? Okay, let's go on.

When the family is divided like this, you don't know the hurt you are putting your mate through. They want to serve God, but you put stumbling blocks in their way. You say, "Stay home with me", or "Let's go somewhere today instead of to worship service." There are many excuses you give your mate. That is all over with now. You *did* go tell your mate you were going to worship, didn't you? Set a goal now that you will never miss any worship service of the church. Now you have applied Matthew 6:33: "But seek ye first the kingdom of God, and his righteousness, and all these things shall be added unto you." We can go on to other goals. But believe me, if God is not your first goal in life, then nothing else matters in life, for all that you gain and obtain in life will be destroyed one day and you will be in hell if you didn't serve God in this life. But I can see you smiling right now because you are serving God, aren't you? And heaven will be your home one day.

Family

The family needs to be a goal for all of us. What good is it if we make all the money in the world, if we do everything for others and neglect our own family? I have a confession to make. I set a goal about five years ago in business which turned out very well. During those five years I worked 60 to 70 hours a week. I went to worship Sunday morning, Sunday night and Wednesday night, and I visited the hospitals on Wednesday afternoons for a few hours. My family was very patient with me and worked hard to help me. If I had not had their support for those five years, I would not be writing this book. Ruby was my beacon for those years. She is the strongest wife, the most caring wife, the most loving wife that anyone could ever ask for. Within those five years I was tired and had it hard many times at work, but she still stood up for me.

I said all that to say this: "I'm pleased that everything worked out the way it did, but I don't think I would do it that way again. Many, many times I would not get home until our boys, Todd and Chad, were asleep. I would go for days without talking to them. I shed tears then, and still do, because my family goal was not before my business goal. Please learn a lesson from my mistake. Set a goal with your family and work hard to obtain it. Once your children grow up, you cannot do all those good things for them that you would like to do. Set a goal to have a family night together. Take that night and just do something together as a family. It doesn't have to be the same night every week. This will take a lot of work because people and things will try to pull you away from it. Another good goal is to really study the Bible together, every night if possible. This goal has helped our family more than anything. We only read one to two chapters a night, and then talk about it a little. Then we pray together. Mostly we pray for the boys, and I'm sure that helps a lot.

Work

This is a good goal for the family to have. How can anyone live without working? (1 Timothy 5:8, "But if any provide not for his own, and especially for those of his own house, he hath denied the faith and is worse than an infidel.") This book is not designed to show you how to move up into better jobs at work, nor does its emphasis concern a lot of other things about work. But one thing it is concerned with, is the setting of goals at work. There are many goals that you can set to have a better job and to make more money. If you will follow these principles, then those things will come naturally.

First, at work (or anywhere as far as that goes), be honest. Next, do the best job you can at work, and you will be rewarded for it. No employer likes a lazy person. If you have a job where you are always away from home, then try to get another one, even if it pays less (and most of the time it will pay less). But what's more important—money or a home? I will take the home any day, won't you?

1 Timothy 6:7 says we brought nothing into this world and we can carry nothing out. We should be content with what we have. Use Paul as an example. He learned to be content. Philippians 4:11, "Not that I speak in respect of want, for I have learned in whatsoever state I am, therewith to be content."

Consider also 1 Timothy 6:8: "And having food and raiment, let us be therefore content."

Goals

1. Name some areas that we can set goals in.

2. What should be our first and main goal in life?

59

3. Why is it important for the family to attend the worship services together?

4. Discuss some goals that you can set with your family.

5. Explain 1 Timothy 5:8.

6. Discuss how the whole family needs to be understanding in this area.

Working Mothers

T he best thing to happen in our lives is that God has given us men a wife. I worship the ground that my wife walks on. We have problems like any other family; we even argue when she doesn't see things the right way (*my* way). I believe without Ruby my life would not be as fulfilling as it is. Ruby helps me in our business more than anyone else. She is much smarter than I am and has more wisdom in decision making. I never make a big decision without asking her advice first. We disagree on some of her advice, but I know it is usually the right thing to do. I know that without Ruby I would not want to live a day longer. I also know that millions of other husbands feel the same way that I do about their own mates. In the business world, I have over 55 women who work for me. They do a very good job. We have a good relationship with all of them. Some of them work because they have to help support their families. Some are not married and work gives them money and something to do. Some of them work to have extra income. Some work and don't have to work. These ladies are not only employees; they are good friends of ours. It hurts us when one leaves, because we like them so well and we want only the best for them. It is good that in this country women can find jobs to support themselves.

The rest of this chapter, you might not agree with. Surely you can see from the beginning that I am not a male chauvinist pig. I believe in women's rights. I will help them to gain them, and I will uphold their rights. I believe that women have the right to work. It's just that I think that too many of them are working when they don't need to. If you don't *need* to work, then please don't work, especially if you have children at home. I don't object to women working outside the home as long as they don't have children at home alone. There are close to two million women every year who are working outside of their homes for the first time. My main objection to this is the women who have children. God has given us these little ones and He expects us to train

and bring them up the right way. Here is what the Bible says about it: (Ephesians 6:4), "And, ye fathers, provoke not your children to wrath, but bring them up in the nurture and admonition of the Lord."

Surely this scripture is telling us to do all we can to bring our children up the right way so God will be pleased. I believe this is the father's and mother's responsibility. I also believe that someone needs to be home all the time that the children are there. The mother does the best job with the children. She can take care of their needs and much better than the father can. A good home-cooked meal or a hug from the mother when the child comes home is worth more than you could ever imagine. (More about this later).

It's a shame in the southern countries like Africa, South America, etc., you see the women doing most of the hard work while the men sit back and watch them. They are not slaves and must not be treated as such.

In America today, since so many women are working outside the home in jobs that pay less then $10,000 to $15,000 a year I wonder how many of them are asking themselves "Is it worth all of this?" I'm sure many are sick and tired of their jobs and would love to be home with their families, even if they only had beans and cornbread to eat. Sometimes it is not what you have that makes you happy, it's what you don't have. Many have the world but don't have the beans and cornbread with their family. I would live on liver and onions (not my favorite dish) the rest of my life, and have a good family life, rather than live on steak and caviar with a bad family situation.

Let us notice some important facts about women working outside the home.

1. In some cases it causes divorce. I realize that this is a bad thing for us to swallow if you are working outside the home, or if you have a wife who works outside the home, but please read on. Here are some reasons why a divorce occurs.

The husband comes home from work. He goes somewhere first to pick up the children. After they arrive home, he begins to open cans to warm up some food for everyone. The children begin to get tired of it before long. The next step is you eat out a lot. Even if it is a hamburger, it costs a lot after a while. At the time, it's worth it. My wife and I worked for four years outside the home. I know that we probably only ate about 250 meals together as a family in those four years. We set goals a lot, and everyone understood that we had to work a lot of hours to accomplish those goals. The main goal was to have our business going well enough so that we would work more for the church and have more time and money to do the things we wanted to do in life. You might be saying that saving money was also part of that goal. If you were raised in a log cabin (not like the fancy ones today) and had to live on $15 to $20 a week as a family, then you might understand why we set those goals. I'm not trying to justify the hours Ruby and I worked outside the home, because we have shed many tears over not spending enough time with our children. Many workaholics may succeed in business, but may fail with their families. You can't call time back. I would give a million dollars today if I could, but I cannot. That is why I am writing this book. It is to help keep you from making the mistakes that I did and to help keep you and men from making them again. So much for the beans and cornbread.

2. Many times when the husband comes home to an empty house and he wants someone to talk to about his day, it is frustrating to find there is no one there. What can he do? Many have turned to other women, to drinking, and whatever else they can find to keep them company. God has set it up for the husband and wife to be together, so please don't try to improve on His works. If you care anything for your marriage, then stay home if you possibly can. I realize that some might be saying "This can't happen to us." I hope it doesn't. If you see a problem like this, then stop it before it breaks up the family.

3. Another reason why a family could break up, is when the wife's job conflicts with activities like fishing, hunting, ballgames, movies, etc. If the mother has to work and the family has to go without her, is the job really worth it? Let me answer that for you. NO! NO! NO!

Day Care

Mothers, where do your children spend their time while you are working? Even if they were at a grandparent's home, did they spend those hours in a playpen, or in someone's arms? Did they get what they wanted when they wanted it? If they are young, did you get to see their first steps, or hear their first words spoken? How sad if you didn't. Does the day care take good care of your child, or do they have 6 to 20 more to care for and don't have time for individual attention? Most of the time this is the case and you know it. A few years ago, people were saying that it is not the quantity of time you spend with your children, it is the quality of time spent. HOGWASH! Nothing will replace the time spent away from your child. Here is a good question to ask your children. "Do you want to go to day care or do you want to stay home with Mother?" I know what the answer to that would be, don't you? When you do leave them at places, are they smiling and telling you goodbye, or are they crying, saying, "Don't go. I want to go with you!"? This makes me cry for you, so I'd better move on.

When the mother works outside the home, they have less time to express their love for their children, and you know this is very important to them. Whoever gets tired of someone telling them that they love them? Or who gets tired of getting a big hug from their mother? You will miss all the playtime together. Children grow up too fast today. We don't let them stay children long enough. Keep them young as long as you can, because they will grow up soon enough. Another problem is when your children get sick and you are at work. No medicine is better then mom's chicken soup, even if it comes out of a can. Mom makes it taste better. You can have grandmother, doctors, day cares, baby sitters, but believe me, NO ONE can take mother's place - especially when they are sick.

Work Alternatives

If you are a mother who must work, let me suggest some alternatives for you. Some mothers *have* to work and some just *want* to work. That's fine, but if you have children at home, please consider these alternatives:

1. *WORK IN THE HOME.* Try to find a job where you can work at home. In this way, you can have the best of both worlds. There are typing jobs that some companies will let you do at home. You might be able to use your phone in a job at home. Many companies are doing this now, especially photography companies. You could have a mail order company in your home. There are many books at the book stores that show you how to set up this type of business, so why not try it? Clothing alterations in the home have always been in great demand. If you don't know how to do this, then learn how. It will be worth it just to stay home with your family, and once you start this bsuiness you will have more work than you can handle. Your friends and customers will keep you so busy that you will wonder why you haven't done this before. If you don't want people coming to your house, then go to an alteration shop. They will give you some of their work to do at home. Or go to the dry cleaners or a clothing store. They will be glad to give you some work to do at home. And you know how long it takes them to do alterations for you!

   There are many other jobs that you can develop at home. Just use your imagination and start looking for the job which will keep you at home with your children. Just think of the money and time you will save by working at home. You can afford to work for less and will end up clearing more money in the long run by working at home. With these types of jobs you can work your schedule around anything that comes up.

2. *WORK ONLY WHILE YOUR CHILDREN ARE IN SCHOOL.* Try to look for a job that will get you back home before your

children arrive there. Also in this type of job, try to work it out to be able to take off to be with your children when they need you. This type of job will be one that doesn't seem like a job. There are many more jobs like this than you can imagine. A few are jobs that sell over the phone, bookkeeping for small businesses, and then there are many housecleaning jobs available. You can work a few hours a day at this and make good money, and you will be your own boss. I know some are saying, "I won't stoop that low." Dear friend, we are talking about saving a marriage, being home with your children, freedom from the world, and doing church work in your spare time. So please try to find anything that will help you to be a better wife and mother. I know a lady who cleans houses and has a family life I would give anything to have.

3. *WORKING A FULL DAY.* This type of work is less desirable for me. I would love to see every mother home with their children, but since at times this is impossible, then you need a job. Try to find one without much pressure - one where you can leave it at work at the end of the day, and not bring work-related problems home with you. Try to find one where they will let you leave to be with your children when they need you.

There are many jobs out there, so before you take one, consider your husband and your children first. If you work all this out first, then you will take care of a lot of problems before they arise. I realize that some of you need to work. I'm not trying to talk you out of it. I am just saying please try and find alternatives to leaving the home for work. You might have to live on less, you might not have the boats and fancy things that your neighbors have, but you will have a family that loves and cares for each other, and believe me, they would give it all up to have what you have.

Working Together

I don't think there is a perfect way for the husband and wife to both work. Since this does happen, however, let me suggest some ideas that will help this to work better. I know that this situation can be worked out, because Ruby and I have this type problem. Ruby doesn't work outside the home because we need the money. She does it because we need her ability to manage one of our businesses. Without her, this one business would probably go down the drain in a short time. She is going to manage it for one more year and then she will stay at home with the children. This is how we have worked it out for the past four years. Anytime one of our children is sick, Ruby or I spend the day with them. My parents live about two miles from our home. They are a big help to us. When we are not with Todd and Chad, they are. They are never left alone at home. We are very thankful for this. My parents clean our house just about every day, and on Fridays we have someone to clean the whole house for us. Usually they have dinner ready for us at our house or theirs about two or three days a week. I usually fix dinner one or two days a week, with Ruby's help, and on Sunday we have a family dinner with my parents after church. All of this takes a lot of pressure off Ruby by the time she comes home. Once she gets home she helps the boys with their homework. She doesn't have to worry about the house or the meals. This schedule doesn't work every week, but it works most of the time for us. The husband and wife must work together if they expect their family to stay together. Each night before we go to bed we try to read a chapter or two from the Bible together around the table. Dear friend, this is the most important thing you can do at home. If you have a schedule to eat, then have a schedule to study the Bible every day.

I can tell you all kinds of ways to help you, but without God's help you will never survive in this present world. If our family didn't rely upon God, then we could never make it. We are not perfect, we need help every day in order to survive in this old world. That's why we put our trust in God.

While we are on the subject of working together, make sure your children are helping, too. Our two boys are 14 and 19 years old. Many times when I have them do something, they do a half-way job to please me. I know I could do it better myself, but I let them do it. They need to build character. The best way to do that is manual labor. If you love your children, you will get them off the couch, away from the T.V.. for a while, and give them something to do. With my boys, I plan one major project every summer for them to do, mostly on their own. It ranges from building a fence to tearing a fence down. If you can do something like this, it will bring your family closer together. You can help them mow yards during the summer to earn money and to build character. Use your own imagination. I am sure you can come up with better things to do than what I have. It will also keep your children from running around all summer and possibly getting into trouble. I don't care what my boys become in life - they can dig ditches, make hamburgers, wash dishes, work on a garbage truck - it doesn't matter to me as long as they serve God, stay out of trouble and do what is right.

Dear friend, while your children are young, that is the time to teach them the right things in life. It is also the time to teach them the most important things in life.

Child Care

While both parents are working outside the home, you need to decide who will be taking care of the children. We have already talked about a day-care program, so I won't get into that again. But with all due respect, let me say that there are a few good day-care programs in this country. The best, in my opinion, are those sponsored by local churches which have a mother's day-out program or a complete program. When looking for someone to take care of your children, try to find someone that you know. Ask people at church who would do a good job. (I said at church, because I cannot imagine you raising children without the church.) Once you have found the right person, try to get them to stay in your home. Some will do this. Here is what you will gain if you do it this way. When you leave, you won't have to wake your child up. They can sleep longer. They won't be crying as much when you leave. They know they are home around their own toys and their own environment. If you drop them off somewhere then they are out of their accustomed environment and don't want to stay there. They feel left out. You might have to go through a few baby sitters to get the right one for your children, so make sure they treat your children as if they were their own. It is hard to determine who will be the best for you. She might be young or old, who knows? The main thing is to make sure she wants to help you and your children.

Working Mothers

1. Discuss mothers working outside the home while they have small children.

2. Do you think that any of these mothers ever ask the question, "Is it really worth me working outside the home?"

3. Could a mother working outside the home result in a divorce? If so, explain how it could.

4. Can you call back the time to do everything over again?

5. Explain the loneliness in a home when the mother is not there.

6. Is it fair to the husband or the children when they have to go places without mom?

7. Why can't a day care take mothers place?

8. What could be some work alternatives?

Working Fathers

F athers, it's good that you have a job and are able to support your family. There are a few things you need to remember:

1. *Don't be a workaholic!* I used to be one, and it really hurt my family life. I still work a lot and have a lot of interest in business, but I try to spend more time everyday with my family I realize now that the time with my family is worth more than the world has to offer. Please learn a lesson from me and take it one day at a time. Don't say, "Next week or next year the family will do this, or that, after I work a while longer." You might not have a family by then.

2. *Don't forget all the work your wife does at home.* Just because you work 40 hours a week, doesn't give you the right to come home and lie around. You can't expect your wife to take your shoes off while you are reading the paper or watching TV. She has worked hard all day, either at home or on a job. You need to help her with the children, cooking, dinner, etc. There are so many things that you must help her with. The best way is to ask her what you can do to be the most help. Then look around and find things that would be helpful. If your wife works out of the home, then remember you are the head of the house (1 Peter 3:5,6), and you must make the house go well. The only way this can happen is if you treat your wife as someone very special. Here is how I do it. I am not ashamed to say that I worship the ground my wife walks on. I would do anything in the world to please her. I realize that I have the best wife in the world, and I must keep her happy. We have our disagreements, but we try to please one another. If you wife doesn't work outside the home, you still must help her and do all you can to please her. The Bible says in 1 Peter 3:7 that we must give honor to the wife. We need to honor them every time that we have the opportunity to do so.

The best way I know to tell you to treat your wife, is to have you read Proverbs 31. This chapter will help you to be thankful for what you have. I am sure there are thousands of people who would like to have what you have, so take care of your wife and treat her right. The Bible tells us in Ephesians 5:25, "Husbands, love your wives, even as Christ also loved the church and gave himself for it." Paul is telling us here that we should love our wives enough to be willing to die for them.

Many husbands want their wives to work outside the home so they can have a new boat, car, etc. They forgot about the children. You might have to work a little harder so your wife won't have to work. There are nearly six million preschool children whose mothers are working outside the home. Do you want that for your children? We don't spend enough time with them now, and much less if we are gone all the time working unnecessarily. If you don't spend time with your children now, then it won't be long before they will leave home and you would give anything to have them back with you. It is so easy to say "tomorrow" or "next week we will do something together." Dear friend, do it *now, today*. Don't put your family off for anything unless it is for church.

Working Fathers

1. What is a "workaholic?"

2. Why is it important to spend time now with our children?

3. Discuss Proverbs 31.

4. Why is it important for a father to help his wife at home, even if she doesn't work outside the home?

TIME OUT

Time Out

This chapter will sound a little different to most of you. As a matter of fact, if you are a Christian, then you will probably disagree with this chapter. If you are a preacher, then the chances are even greater that you will disagree with this chapter. But I believe if you will read it with an open mind, then you will see what I am trying to say, and I believe that one day you will agree with me. I believe that God has to be first with us. But what bothers me is that we expect a person to teach a Bible class for the rest of their lives without a time out. We expect a person to visit the sick without a time out. We expect a person to go door-knocking without a time out. We expect a person to work all day long, seven days a week for the Lord without a time out, plus do the hundreds of other things he has to do. Well, as I said, God has to be first in our lives. *But we do wrong by not taking a time out.*

Leisure time was important to God, to Christ, and it must be important to us, also. I believe that we feel guilty when we are not working ourselves to death. I used to feel that way, and I'm trying to get away from it. It is hard to have leisure time once you have worked hard all your life. If we don't take time out to enjoy some leisure time, then before long we will be too old to enjoy any leisure time at all. We live in a society where we think we must work 10 to 12 hours a day, and then come home and work an additional 4 or 5 hours. Well, it is hard to change society, but we can change our own life. And it is up to us to decide what kind of life we want to live.

Isn't it strange when you meet someone for the first time - after you tell them your name, the first thing they ask is where you work, and where your mate works. This is the real world in which we live. Ruby and I both work outside the home and now we can choose our hours. But I believe that it would be much better if one of us were at home. If for no other reason than to relax and enjoy the life of peace and quiet while no one else is home during the day. I look forward to the day when someone asks me my name, and then, "How does your wife enjoy her leisure time at home?" (I know a woman's work is never done at home. She has a lot to do.) I long to see that day in everyone's lives. We have gotten so busy making money for ourselves and our children, that we don't have time to give them the important things in life - time, love, leisure. I am convinced after looking over my life and lives of others, that it is essential for us to have leisure time.

No Time Out

Isn't it strange that most of us (especially men), think that we cannot take a time-out from work? How many of us take work home with us to finish at night? Well, stop it! If you can't get it done in eight hours, then let it go until the next day. If you are reading this book and you are an employer, then stop right now expecting your employees to take work home with them. They have a home life. If you want them to be better employees, then help them to have a better family life. As a matter of fact, try to do things for their family if you can, and you will notice how much better they will perform their job. You will also notice their positive attitude at work.

To be a good employer, you must respect your employee's family life. Don't call them back in to work unless you really cannot make it without them. I have people who work for me who tell me, "If you need any help, then give me a call at home." They know that I will never call them unless it is an absolute emergency. They need a *time out* from work, and a *time out* with their families.

Have you ever taken a vacation and while packing, you get a lot of things together to "work on" while you are away? Well, stop that! A vacation is a time to get away from work and not a time to continue it. It is all right to read and study while on vacation, but be ready to give it up as soon as anyone in that family wants you to do something with them. Don't say, "Wait until I read more or study more.' Go right then!

Leisure time is a "must" for our lives. I thought at one time that no one should have leisure time — that it was wasteful. I still have a problem with it, and I'm working on my leisure time (no pun intended). We who are Christians can see the importance of time and we want to do all we can for the Lord before we die. We might just die before we can do all we planned to do for the Lord. What I mean by this is, that if we don't take a time out from time to time, then we might very well be shortening our lives and not live long enough to do all the things that we would have liked to do. Even Jesus saw the importance of a time out. Look at Mark 6:30-32: "And the apostles gathered themselves unto Jesus, and told him all things, both what they had done, and what they had taught. And he said unto them, come ye yourselves apart into a desert place, and rest awhile: for there were many coming and going, and they had no *leisure* so much as to eat. And they departed into a desert place by ship privately."

You see, if Jesus could see the importance in leisure time, then so must we. Don't you think so? I believe that if we expect to survive in this present world, then we must have some leisure time. I also realize that a person who works at a desk job all day can have leisure time digging fence holes, and a person who digs fence holes all day can have leisure time sitting at a desk. So a person must decide on his own what relaxes him the most, and go for it. Also, we need to have different ways of relaxing. Leisure time should be spent doing things that you like to do. All work and no play will make you sick at the end of your life. I wish I could interview a million people who already have their families raised and are home alone. I believe that the majority of them would say they would give anything if they had played more with their family and worked less at their job. I believe that a family is much more important, don't you? If you do, then begin today spending more time with your family. Take more time out for leisure time. We all have plans when we retire, but now is the time to do things with our family because once we retire, our children will have their own families, and we won't be able to do many things with them then.

Time Out

1. Can we be wrong in not taking time out from things that keep us so busy?

2. Why do we feel guilty when we take time out?

3. Why is leisure time important to us?

4. What can we gain by leisure time?

5. Instead of trying to change society's way of thinking, where would be a better place to begin?

6. Why do you think that time seems to be going faster every year? Why do we seem unable to slow it down?

7. Why do we need a "Time Out" from work?

8. Discuss Mark 6:30-32.

THE BEAUTY OF
GRANDPARENTS

The Beauty Of Grandparents

I f God has blessed you enough to be a grandparent, then this chapter and this book should help you in finding the beauty of age.

I always set goals, and I work hard to accomplish them. One goal that I have in life is to grow old. I don't want to die young. I don't want people to look at me at my funeral and say, "He sure died young. Look how good he looks." I want people to say, "Wow, he sure lived a long life!" I want them to say, "Bill and Ruby were the best grandparents that ever lived." I want them to say, "They sure loved young people." Isn't it sad when older people get a reputation of being mean and not liking young people? I pray that I will always have a love for young people.

I realize that I'm not a grandparent yet. I'm old enough to be one, so one day I pray God will bless Ruby and me with grandchildren. You are probably thinking, "If he is not a grandparent, then he can't tell us anything." I don't want to tell you anything. I just want to let you know what grandparents, grandchildren and the in-between are going through. Maybe it will help you to see the beauty of grandparents.

Children

First, let me start with what I have noticed in life concerning grandparents. Our parents are ideal. They help us at home in keeping the house clean, cooking meals and repairing things. I don't know what we would do without our parents. They will do anything in the world for us. They have always been available to babysit our boys. We can depend on them anytime of the day or night. If you are a grandparent, then you need to have some of these qualities. If you want your children to always love you, then keep your children happy and do all you can for them.

Now those of us who are children, we need to take care of our parents. Listen to what Paul told Timothy in 1 Timothy 5:8: "But if any provide not for his own, and especially for those of his own house, he hath denied the faith, and is worse than an infidel." You see, if you claim to be a Christian and don't take care of your family, then you, my friend, are in bad shape according to the word of God. If our parents need or want something, then we should do all we can to get it from them. Once we marry, we leave the home, but we don't leave our parents. We must help them in every way that we can. We won't have them long, so now is the time to give them flowers. Don't wait until they are dead and gone. I am sure many sons and daughters will shed many tears now becuase they didn't tell their parents they loved them, and they didn't prove their love for them before they died. It takes a special couple to understand and prove their love for parents and parents-in-law. Won't you have that special love today and do all you can for them.

Parents, remember that they are your children's grandparents. Give them plenty of time together. Don't be selfish with your children. Share them. We let our boys spend Friday nights with their grandparents when they want to. This helps all three of us. The grandparents spend time with them. They buy them junk food; they sit up late on Friday night and have a good time. The grandchildren have a good time. They get away from us, and they need that from time to time. Ruby and I think we get the best part of the deal. We can go out and eat, or just stay at home and listen to *nothing*. It is so peaceful to hear nothing. No T.V., no radio, no children making noise - just plain old nothing. A few parents won't let their children visit their grandparents because of disagreements. If that is your case, then repent today and ask God to forgive you so you can be a family again. Now let's go to the grandchildren!

Grandchildren

Grandchildren, you are the luckiest people in the world. You have many people who love and care for you. When you were born, you had parents and grandparents who cried when that joyful occasion took place. They were so happy that you were here and could not hold back the smiles and tears, for they thought you were the most beautiful baby in the world. They still think of you that way. When you get into trouble, your parents and grandparents still love you.

Grandchildren, don't ever let your grandparents down. They think you hung the moon. When you are tempted to do wrong, think of your grandparents. Think of how it would break their hearts if you got into bad trouble. Let me tell you a few things that will help you see the beauty in your grandparents. Always see the good in the things they do. If you disagree with them, *never, never* talk back to them. And *never, never* say an unkind word to them. You won't have your grand-parents for long, so love them in a very special way while you have them. A few people don't even have grandparents. I don't. So take good care of them, okay?

Grandchildren, you need to remember that your parents are in charge of you. Don't have your grandparents and your parents divided over things you want them to do. Your parents have the final say, so take heed. (Ruby says that word is a word with a bark to it, whatever that means).

Grandchildren, don't be asking your grandparents for everything you see. Many do not have the money to buy a lot of things. They are on a limited income and do not have a lot of extra money. It is so hard for them so say "no" to you, but I know that you would not want them doing without things they want or need in order to indulge your selfishness. There are many ways you can be of assistance to them. Mow the lawn, help paint the house, go to the store for them. Think up a lot of things that you can do for them, and do it!

Grandparents

If you are a grandparent, then God has blessed you more than you will ever know. While your children were growing up, you had to work and make a living for them. You are writing this book. You are the most beautiful people in the world. You can play with your grand-children and then send them home when they are acting up. Oh, how I would like to be in your shoes at times.

Grandparents, you are blessed to see your children and grand-children mature and achieve their goals in life. All this time you can say they are a part of you. Only a grandparent can have this joy in life. You need to find all the joy you can with your grandchildren, for James said in James 4:14, "Whereas ye know not what shall no the morrow. For what is your life? It is even a vapour, that appeareth for a little time, and then vanisheth away."

Life is very short, so you must spend time, love, and money with your grandchildren. Take time to make them things, like a wooden sword, sling shot, swing, etc. There are many things that you can make for them that I don't even know about, so start today. A good thing is to help them make a gift for their parents. Help them carve out a duck decoy or something like that. By doing this, you will have three people who will be closer together. The gift will be cherished forever. By the way, if any of my grandchildren ever read this book, I collect duck decoys and smiles. I don't know which I like best.

Sooner or later you will say, "How fast the years have gone." When this happens, make sure that you spent those first years one day at a time with your grandchildren. My children see their grandparents five to seven days a week. By the way, we all worship together at the East Side Church of Christ in Cleveland, Tenneessee. Won't you come and worship with us sometime? We need one more to make up our family at the great East Side. You need to make the most of your time, make every day count for the good with your grandchildren.

While they visit in your home, treat them like Kings and Queens. Do anything for them. When they act up, and give you a hard time, lay it on them. Make them mind you when they are in your home. If you don't, then you will spoil them rotten. They will take advantage of you and treat you like a dog. (No offense to a dog; some dogs eat better than I do.)

Plan things to do with your grandchildren. Take them to ball games, restaurants, shopping, hunting and fishing, camping, etc. I'm sure you can think up things to do. So start thinking and doing. I told Ruby that within the next week or two, I am going to buy two rocking chairs to put on the front porch. I plan on making plans every night in that rocking chair. Most of those plans will be concerning our grandchildren. This book should be published within 10 or 12 months. When you read this, come by and rock with me. I hope to have the rocking chair broken in by that time. I believe you and I can solve a lot of problems by prayer and thinking in the old rocking chair. Never waste time, even when sitting around the house. Use your mind to help you become a better grandparent. Don't try to live more than one day at a time. If you put things off for another day, then that day may never come.

To be the best grandparent that ever lived (and I'm sure that is what you want to be), then you need to take a lesson from the best people in life. Why do you think Moses prayed for forty days and forty nights? To solve a problem! Why did Jeremiah stand up for God? To solve a problem. Why did Paul preach to all the world? To solve a problem. Why did Jesus die on the cross? To solve a problem. I said all that to say this: if you want to be the best grandparent, if you want to help solve your problems with your children and grandchildren, then spend much time alone with God. I cannot imagine doing anything without God's help, can you?

The Beauty Of Grandparents

1. Explain 1 Timothy 5:8.

2. Why is it important to be good to our grandparents and parents now?

3. How can grandchildren break their grandparent's heart?

4. In light of James 4:14, why should grandparents do all they can for their grandchildren?

5. Why should grandparents make their grandchildren mind them?

WHY FAMILIES AREN'T
CLOSE TODAY

Why Families Aren't Close Today?

O ne of the best things that we will ever have in this life is a family. A family is a group of people who will stay together even if the world is against them. As long as a family stays together, they can overcome any obstacle which may get in their way. They can overcome temptation and they can enjoy life. The problem is when a family is no longer close. How sad it is when a family is divided. How sad it is when they go their separate ways because they can't agree. How sad it is when they argue and fight within the family. I confess to you that my family is not perfect, and I don't believe that anyone has a perfect family. But I do know that we all need to work at getting our families closer together, before the distance between them is too far to be repaired. Let me suggest some things I believe are causing families not to be close today. Some of these I have already talked about in this book. But I need to mention a few of them again to show you how important it is to keep the family close today.

1. Pleasures of life divide the family.
2. Television divides the family.
3. Work divides the family.
4. School divides the family.
5. Friends can cause division.
6. Church can sometimes divide the family.
7. Being too busy divides the family.

Pleasures Of Life Divide The Family

We live in a world today in which we and our children think we must have a certain type of clothing in order to be acceptable. A new car. A new home. Toys everywhere. Lots of money. We are anxious to give our children all these things and more. It seems strange to me that today the father and mother work outside the home to give our children all these things and all they really want and need is for us to spend time with them. Somehow we as parents have failed to give our children the best things in life. By the way, you cannot buy the best things in life. They are free of charge. James tells us in James 1:17, "Every good gift and every perfect gift is from above, and cometh down from the Father of lights, with whom is no variableness, neither shadow of turning." God gives *everyone* the best things in life, but we try to improve on them and end up giving our children things that are not always the best for them.

I don't know how we can stop the world from being so in love with the pleasures of life. But I do know that it must begin at home, where we are right now. If we could accomplish the goal of living for pleasures, then it has to keep our families together. Let me suggest some ways that might help.

1. *Birthdays.* Don't give your children a lot of gifts. One or two small gifts would be fine. Too many times they expect too much and they go from one gift to another, without even appreciating them.

2. *Christmas.* At our home we don't celebrate Christmas as Christ's birthday. But we do enjoy the holiday, and we give gifts. This would be a good time not to give as much to each other. Not only would you help your children to appreciate the few things they get, but it will save you a lot of money. During this time of the year, parents are sad because they can't give their children more than they can afford. Well, dear friend, just give them love and time, and that will be more important than anything you could buy with money.

3. *Shopping.* During the year while shopping, be wise enough to tell your children "No!" when they want everything they see. Don't give in! Some children pitch fits in stores for toys. They don't need a toy, they need a good slap on their rear. I'm not saying never to give children toys. I'm just saying that they should not expect them every time you go shopping.

4. *Grandparents.* Make sure the grandparents don't give the grandchildren everything they see and want. Some grandparents will give them anything they ask for. Stop this situation before it goes too far.

5. I hope that you can think of a lot more things that will keep you from giving your children everything they want. If we expect them to grow up and be good citizens, then it takes good training while they are young.

I have noticed that many young couples want everything their parents have. They don't realize that their parents worked for 20 or 30 years to obtain what they now have. I believe most of this is because we give them too much while they are growing up. I also believe it is the cause of many failed marriages among the young. It is difficult for these young couples to struggle to make homes for themselves and to pay their bills and build a home, when they are accustomed to everything being handed to them. I must confess that I give my boys a lot of pleasures in life. Sometimes I give them things without any reason at all. Well, I'm trying to improve on this and I hope you are too.

Another thing that might help us as parents is to watch what we want and buy in life. If we want a lot, then our children will want a lot. If we could only be content with less in this life, then I believe that our children will be content with less. I believe that it is up to us parents to set the example for our children. I find myself buying items that I don't really need. The problem with this is that my boys see this and in their minds they think they can do the same thing. Not everyone can handle money and maybe our children won't be able to handle it as well as we can. So we as parents need to teach our children to do without things, and by all means teach them to save for a rainy day. If they don't save a little money, then they will have it hard the rest of their lives. I would advise all young people to put aside about five per-cent of their wages every week in the bank, stocks, or some type of in-vestment. By doing this they will learn to live on less and at the same time they will be investing in their future. If they continue this, then within 20 or 30 years of working they will be able to retire with a good income.

The pleasures of life have caused more families to break up than anything else. If we expect our families to stay together, then we must be content with what we have. I'm not saying that a Christian cannot have any of the things of this life. It is just that we must not be a group of people who are always wanting more and never content with what we have in life. I can tell you from experience that contentment is not in the pleasures of life - it is a state of mind to be satisfied with what we have. A good friend of mine, Claiborne Kerr, said they have anything they want in life. It's just that they don't want much! If all of us could be like my good friend, then this would be a better world to live in.

Television Divides The Family

I have already written a chapter in this book on television, so I won't talk too much about this. I do believe that the television is dividing the family today. The reason why is that the television is keeping the family from being close, because it monopolizes so much of our time. Most families have a T.V. in every room. You have a child in one room, and parents in another room, watching different programs. Television could be better if we only had one in the house and set aside a certain time for the family to watch it together. By doing this, the parents can monitor what the family watches. If it is a bad program, then the parents will be there to turn it off, and to explain why. If we could just set a rule that the television would not be on until the family can be together and watch it, I feel it could be a great thing. But the sad part is that as soon as we come into the house, we turn on the T.V., even before we take our coat off. The T.V. will be playing while we are in another room, and how many times have you come home and found that you left it on while you were away from home? If you have a television, then I suggest that you put it in a place where it will be hard to get to, like the basement, or in a room where you don't spend much time. As a matter of fact, I'm considering putting our T.V. in a closet just to make it uncomfortable for us, so we won't spend a lot of time in front of it.

Work Divides The Family

Family businesses are the most ideal situations that I know of. Many of them don't work out very well, but the ones that do work out are very rewarding to the family. There are many advantages of a family business. If there is any way that you can begin one, I suggest that you do so. A lot of good businesses have started with the family in a basement or garage. There are a lot of good books out concerning this, so go to the book store and look around. If you try one and it fails, then try another.

Since the majority of people don't have a family business, we all need to work really hard on spending more time together, and less at work. I'm not saying you should quit your job and lie around the house, because I don't believe that would work either. But I am saying you should *not* bring your work home with you!

I have a good friend who is an executive for G.M. I asked him one day why he didn't bring a brief case home from work. He said that G.M. doesn't want their employees to bring their work home. They want you to work while you are there, and forget about it while you are home. I admire G.M. and other companies for this because the job is not worth destroying the family. A company would do better if they would realize that its employees have a family life and let them live it. At times a lot of companies believe that the job comes first and the family last. I disagree with that concept. I believe that if the family is happy, then they will do a better job at work.

To keep the family together, I believe there will be times in life when people need to turn down a promotion, which most of the time has a raise to go along with it. I realize that you are thinking that I am crazy. But think about it! With many promotions comes more responsibility, more time away from the family, and possibly even making a move to another location. Money and power aren't everything. As a matter of fact, I believe that money and power are nothing, and at times they are stumbling blocks to our having a happy family.

Let me give you an example. If one family makes a hundred dollars a week and cannot afford a television and fancy things, they spend time talking together, playing games, working together around the house, in the garden, etc. This also encourages a positive and happy attitude, and allows our love for one another to grow. Maybe this family also has to make their own clothing, sell vegetables out of the garden, etc., in order to earn a little extra money. Now another family makes $1,000 a week. They have a television in every room, with everyone watching something different. They have anything they want, but they still want more. They don't talk much to each other. They don't play any games together. They hire someone to do all the work around the house. They have a negative attitude and always complain and are never satisfied. They buy the best things in life. They go their separate way; they don't eat together and don't do much of anything together. Now which family do you think you would rather be like? I would rather be like the one who makes $100 per week, because power and money are nothing. I hope this example will help you because we all get so caught up in the world that we don't see the important things in life.

There are a lot of things that we will never understand about life. One of those things is the desire to work and succeed in life. All through history many have had a desire to succeed in life. The part that I can't understand is why do most of us neglect our family in order to succeed in life? Is this truly successful. We might gain things of the world, but without a family to share them with, we are not a success. Life is hard enough the way it is. Without a family to work and share with, I don't seehow any of us can make it. Isn't it strange how we spend a lot of extra time at work so we can give a lot to our children, and by the time we can give them a lot, they are already grown up and gone. I guess we just have everything backwards in life. In a way, it would be good if we could spend a lot of time with our family while they are young, and once they leave home, then we can work a lot. But I guess no solution is perfect. We just need to try and work on being a good family unit.

Friends Divide The Family

Friends are one of the best things we could ever have in this life. Friends are one thing that we can never have too many of. A friend is someone who will stay with you even when everyone else has left you. All of us need friends. One thing that we need to remember about friends is that we can spend more time with them than with our families if we aren't careful. Many families are divided because a husband thinks he needs to go out with "the boys" every night and leave the family at home. Or the wife thinks she needs to go out with "the girls" every night while the family stays home. This cannot be. Your family needs to come before your friends. Good friends will not try to divide the family. They will know when to be there and when not to be around.

This problem usually arises with newly married couples. It will be a hard thing to stop going out so much with the boys. Many of them won't understand because they are not married themselves. Once they get married they will be able to better understand. So until they do, you have to have patience with them. You don't need to give them up as friends; you just need to understand that your mate comes before them.

Young couples need also to make sure the confidence they put in their friends is not abused. They do not need to tell them all about their problems at home. And by all means, no one needs to choose sides when you and your mate have a disagreement. It will be so easy to tell your friends all about your problems at home, and they, in many cases, will give you the wrong advice. They only hear one side of the story. Until we hear both sides, we cannot give the best advice. If we really care about our friends we will mind our own business and try not to give too much advice to our friends.

There will be many times in life when our friends will want us to do things with them, and we will have to tell them "no" because we need to spend that time with our family. This hurts, but it must be done. The way that I have solved that problem is I hardly go anywhere without Ruby or the boys. When someone wants me to go snow skiing with them, I ask them if Ruby can come along. If not, then I usually tell them I couldn't have a good time without her, so I'd rather not go this time. When someone wants me to go hunting or fishing with them, I ask them if Todd or Chad can go with us. If not, then I usually tell them that I couldn't have a good time without my boys. If we can practice this type of attitude, then I believe that our friends won't divide our family. By the way, if I go anywhere and spend the night without my family, I may as well sit up all night, because I can't sleep. Many people aren't affected in this manner because their jobs require them to travel, or whatever. That doesn't mean they love their family any less than I do; it's just that I don't have to travel without some of my family, and I choose not to go anywhere without at least part of my family with me.

School Divides The Family

I am sure some of you are saying, "How in the world can school divide the family?" I thought the same thing until I realized how the school taxes our children with all it's various activities. I believe that it is good that the school offers activities. I would be the first to stand up for it. But it seems in the last few years that there are so many activities at school that the family doesn't have much time together. And any time the family doesn't have time together, there will be problems. Let me give you some examples of what I am referring to. Let's say your son or daughter is in the band. In this town they expect them to practice every day after school. They practice on most Saturdays. They have band competition about twice a month during the school year. They have a band camp during most of the summer. This makes it hard on the family as far as taking a vacation together. They are under pressure, because if they don't practice they don't get to march. I love the band, but I believe the school expects too much out of its members. With all the pressure they have, it makes it hard on the rest of the family.

Let me give you one more example, although I could give you many. Take baseball, for instance. I love baseball, hot dogs, apple pie and Chevrolet, but this is one thing that causes the family to be divided. Now before I go any further, let me remind you that if you have a child who participates in school activities, then you need to go to their games and practices just so you can spend more time together and be involved with their activities. Now, let's get back to baseball. The school expects them to practice just about every night. They play games two or three times a week. They have tournaments about every other weekend. They have ball camps in the summer for them. With all of this, it takes them away from the family. It used to be that the schools would never have anything scheduled on Wednesday nights, because that was Bible study night. Now it's just another night. Activities were never scheduled on Sunday at one time, but now activities extend through the entire weekend.

Now that I have said all that, let me give you my pet peeve about school activities. I believe they should try to win the ballgames, but it has gotten so that we want to win more than we want to play. I believe we have lost the fun of games. Only the best get to play—from grade school on up to pro-ball. What a shame we won't let everyone play! Many kids would love to participate, but the coaches won't let them because they aren't good enough. To me it is so degrading for a boy or girl to sit on the bench just because a coach wants to win another game so badly that he won't let everyone play. If you are a coach and are reading this book, let me suggest one thing to you. Make sure that in every game you let every child play, even for just a short while. If you don't do this, as far as I'm concerned, you are a rotten coach!

Church Divides The Family

I know you are saying that Bill has gone overboard by saying that the church divides the family. Before you stop reading this book, please read the rest of what I have to say. I believe that you will agree with me.

The church has activities for junior high students, teenagers, young adults, middle age adults, older people and any other group we can think of. The church has retreats for these different age groups. The church has summer camps for these group members. Can you see where all this leads? The family is going in ten different directions to keep up with the activities that the church has. I agree that we need activities with the church. As a matter of fact, I promote many of the activities. The thing that bothers me the most is that we don't have enough activities for the *entire* family together. And the best way to do that is not to have the family going on a family retreat with the church? A long time, (if ever), I'll bet. It's up to the leaders of the church to plan things that will keep the family together, because if the family is divided, then before long the church will be divided. I'm not saying that the church is a social institution, but I am saying that the church needs to be together more often than just on Sundays. And when they come together for *anything,* it needs to be with the whole family, if at all possible.

Being Too Busy Divides The Family

This is probably the number one problem with the family today. It seems like people today live too fast a pace of life. Here is how a typical day in America goes. Dad works till five or six, mom works till five or six; then they come home. Mom picks up the baby at the sitter's house on the way home. By the time they get home their teenage boy and girl are home from school and have already left to go to their job at a grocery store or a fast food place. They grabbed a sandwich on their way to work. Mom and dad fix something quick to eat, or they go out to eat, or they eat something they stopped and picked up on the way home. Dad watches television while mom plays with the baby, runs around doing a load of laundry and picking up around the house.

They go to bed before their teenagers get home from work most of the time. On an average day the family won't have 10 minutes together in which everyone is present. You might be saying that this is an exaggeration.

My friend, look at your family life, your neighbor's and your friend's lives, and see if I am right. I don't know the answer on how to slow this world down, but I do know that if we want time for the family, then we have to make time for it. We need to see what is the most important thing for us. Is the family important, or everything else? We can be so busy today that we forget about our own families. This is wrong, and we must work very hard to change it.

Why Families Aren't Close Today?

1. How can the pleasures of life divide the family?

2. Discuss buying things that we don't need, and how our children can easily develop this habit.

3. How can a job divide the family?

4. What are some ways that the television divides the family?

5. How can friends divide the family?

6. Can school divide the family? Explain.

7. Do you believe that even the church can divide the family? Explain.

8. Can we be too busy for our own good?

DIVORCE

Divorce

This is the saddest chapter I have ever written. How sad it is when two people who at one time loved each other so much that they would die for one another, decide to part company for life. The day that Ruby tells me she wants a divorce, or the day that I tell her I want a divorce - if there is no way we can work things out, I pray that God will take my life right then. I cannot imagine living one day without my precious Ruby. We took our vows seriously when we said "until death do us part."

Many good mothers have put up with terrible mates just because they took their vows seriously. I am pleased that this is not our case. But I admire those who keep a marriage together. I am sure many children have said, "Mother, leave dad. He beats you, he drinks, he does everything wrong." Then the mother says, "Children, I take my vows seriously. I will stay with your father, and try to change him by my example." Praise God for mothers like this. They could take the easy way out and leave him, but then the children would not have a father. Then you get into all kinds of trouble. In a Christian marriage, love will not insist on having its own say, but it will insist on serving the other. With this type of attitude, a marriage will not end up in a divorce. In a divorce, we expect the other person to change, and when they don't we want a divorce. Take time and change *yourself* first before you expect a change from your mate. What does it take to see a smile on everyone's face? A smile from you. What does it take to see a positive person? You be positive. You see, if we want others to treat us well, then we must treat them well. I remember hearing and being impressed with Luke 6:31: "And as ye would that men should do to you, do ye also to them likewise." If you think that divorce is no big thing and that it is no big deal for most children, then listen to this. Today there are more than 13 million children under the age of 18 who are without one or both parents. There are more than one million children each year involved in divorce cases. Why don't people think about their children before they commit the terrible act of divorce?

Before you even think about a divorce, make sure that you try everything possible to prevent it. If you have to forgive your mate a hundred times, then do it, and don't get a divorce. If you are determined to get a divorce, let me tell you what God's word has to say about it first. Matthew 19:9 says, "And I say unto you, whosoever shall put away his wife, except it be for fornication, and shall marry another, committeth adultery: and whoso marrieth her which is put away doth commit adultery."

Now here is what that is saying. The only way that anyone can have a divorce is through fornication. The word "fornication" relates to homosexuality, lesbians, men with animals, etc. But the primary meaning is when a mate is involved in a sex act with someone else, other than their own mate. Once this occurs, a person can have a scriptural divorce. But I have often wondered what would cause a person to go out on their mate. Do you think at times they were treated badly and possibly lost all acts of love with them? When this happens, I wonder who caused the guilty party to go out on their mate. Although they have a right to divorce, don't you think it would be much better to forgive and stay together? I think so. But each person has to make this decision on his own.

Another thing that you must watch for concerning Matthew 19:9 is that if you even marry a person who was put away for adultery, then you also commit adultery. So make sure that you don't marry someone who was put away for adultery. Many people marry someone that they do not know very well. If you ever find yourself wanting to marry someone who has been married before, then my friend, it is your duty to find out everything you can about that person. They might tell you anything, or they might keep silent about a former marriage. It is up to you to visit the person's family and friends and ask a lot of questions about the former marriage. If that person whom you want to marry doesn't have a scriptural reason for divorce, and you marry him, then you will be guilty of Matthew 19:9. To put it bluntly, hell will be waiting for you. Nothing, or no one in this world is worth going to hell over. There may be times when you are not sure if the person is living in adultery. Take the safe route and don't marry that person. I am sure that some of you are saying, "What about just dating that person, without plans for marriage?" My advice to you is to stay away from that person, because in God's eyes they are still married to their former mate. I don't care what the law of the land says about this. There is a higher law and that is God's law. How can anyone date another person's mate? You can't do that, and do that which is right. Maybe if you stayed away from that person, they might

96

go back to their former mate where they should be. But as long as you are in the picture, then it will be hard on that person to go back and try to salvage their marriage.

Divorce At An Old Age

I have see people go through just about everything together, and once they reach an older age, and should be spending peaceful, happy years together, they get a divorce. What causes this? I really don't know if anyone has the answer to this, but I know a few things that will prevent a marriage from breaking up in old age.

First, while you are young, stay in love with your mate. Worship the ground they walk on. Always treat them special. While you have children at home, don't forget and neglect your mate. Go out once a week on a date. This habit, if started early, will continue long after the children have left home.

Second, try to find a hobby that both of you like. I like to hunt and fish, but Ruby doesn't. Ruby likes to shop. So when I go hunting or fishing, I find a place that has a good shopping center with lots of stores. This way, we do our own thing, but are together while on the trip. A good hobby that Ruby and I have is eating. We don't eat too much, we just like to eat. Through this hobby, we have many friends join us. We go out many times with our friends to different restaurants. Try to find hobbies that both of you like, and it will make your marriage last "until death do you part." And isn't that what you vowed to one another in the begining of your marriage?

A third and most important thing that will help you to keep your marriage together is to have the church in common. With both of you being Christians, trying your best to serve God, then you will be able to work your problems out. I really don't see how any marriage could stay together without God being one of the main sources of strength. It is a hard life just to exist here on earth. If you ever expect to make it, then I encourage you to make sure that both of you are Christians and are putting God first in your life. If you need any help in becoming a Christian, then read these five scriptures: Mark 16:16; Luke 13:3; Romans 10:10; Acts 2:38; Matthew 28:18-20. Also, if I can help you in any way, then please let me know.

Fourth, let your children have their own life. If you are all the time involved in their lives, then before you know it, you will be hurting your own marriage. Don't give them any advice unless they ask for it. Everyone has and will always have problems, so just think about your own, and let others do the same. If you can help them, and they want you to, then go ahead. But remember that you also have a marriage to work with and to strengthen.

Divorce

1. In order to prevent divorce, who should be first to try to change things at home for the better?

2. Discuss Luke 6:31.

3. Why is a divorce so hard on the children?

4. According to Matthew 19:9, what is the only reason for a divorce?

5. Think about this before you answer it. What would cause a person to go out on their mate and to commit fornication?

6. Why is it important to take our marriage vows seriously?

7. Why are mutual hobbies important?

8. How can the church help in a marriage?

The Empty Nest

I don't know who originally entitled this subject as an "empty nest," but they sure did title it correctly. Once the children have left home, we certainly have an empty spot, both in our homes and in our hearts. It seems like we humans go through stages in life, and this is probably the hardest of them all. What do we do with our time once the children have left home? This could be the best years of our lives, or the hardest. These years of retirement should be well-planned for, long before we reach retirement. I hope to retire in a few years from business, but I am already making plans for another career. I plan on spending another 40 years conducting revivals and working with a church as an elder or minister. I don't know what the Lord holds in store for me, but I plan on doing His will. I hope you are making plans right now for your retirement. If you wait until that day arrives before you make plans, then your marriage will suffer and so will you. I believe that since a large number of people are getting divorced after 20 years of marriage, a big contributing factor is the fact that they did not plan for the empty nest. Many couples wrap themselves entirely around their children for so many years and do not spend time with one another. After the children are gone, they find that they are living with a stranger. Please, please spend time with your spouse. Develop a deep, loving, and strong relationship with your mate. This will better equip you for the time when the children have gone to pursue careers and lives of their own.

Let us notice a few things about the empty nest that I hope will help all of us once we have an empty nest, and maybe we can help those who already are faced with this emptiness. In the following chapter we will talk about these subjects:

1. The Children Aren't Coming Home
2. The Home Will Be Silent And Different The Rest Of Your Life
3. You Need To Renew Your Love For Each Other
4. You Need A Hobby - Lots Of Them!

5. You Need The Church
6. Don't Stay Bored - Do Something!
7. Help Other People (Especially Those Facing The Same Emptiness)
8. Helping The Empty Nest To Be A Great Place To Live.

The Children Aren't Coming Home

How sad these words are. What a terrible feeling this must be. We have two boys, ages 14 and 19, and it won't be long before they will leave the nest. I dread it more than anything. I wish they could stay under our protection, our guidance, our home life forever. But I know that would not be good for them, or for us. It brings tears to my eyes just thinking about these little boys going out into the big world all alone. While they are home, and especially a year or two before they leave the nest, we must instill in their minds that we will always be there to help them. Not to interfere in their business, but to lend a helping hand. They need to know also that they will always have a home with us. Too many times young people leave home and would give anything to come back. But they feel they are no longer welcome. I hope my children never feel that way. The fact is once they get married and establish their own nest, then they are not coming home to live again. The sooner we accept that the better off they will be. There will be many times that they will need money, or just someone to talk to as a friend, and we need to be there for them.

Once the children have left home, the mother and father need to start a new way of life. We cannot live in the past. We cannot control what has already been done, but we can get on with our lives and that is what *we* must do. We have got to find things to do that will help to occupy our time. Look around at other people and see the lives they live. If you like it, then do it as long as it is nothing wrong or sinful. Some people like to sit on the front porch and rock in their rocking chair all day long. The only way I could do that is to read or find something for my hands to do. I believe that we should keep busy producing things (even if it is only carving out a toy for the children) for the rest of our lives.

Just because we have an empty nest doesn't mean that it has to be "empty". We need to think of things to do every day of our life. It is not much of a life to eat, sleep and watch T.V. all day long. I know there are things that everyone can do once they have an empty nest. We just need to think of them and work on them. Since the children are not coming home to live again, now is a good time to make things for them. You can make quilts, ceramics, furniture, clothing, ties, work on their house, work outside their homes on the lawn, etc. You can make toys for your grandchildren, take them places such as hunting, fishing, etc. There are thousands of things that you can do just for your immediate family and for those around you. Oh yes, you can also make them a cake or pie, or just any type of food. Our parents help us with all the above, and we really do appreciate it!

The Home Will Be Silent, And Different
For The Rest Of Your Life

Once the children leave home, you will miss them more than you ever have in your life. It is one thing for children to go somewhere and then come back home. But it's altogether different when they leave home, and you know they are not coming back to live with you. At times I wish my boys could live with us forever, but I know that God has designed it for them to leave home. We as parents need to make the home a good place for them to be and once they leave home, they will want to return to visit many times. It is so sad when a child leaves home and says, "I will never return here because of the way I was treated while I was here." We all need to make sure that our children will want to come home.

I have been making plans for a few years to do things with my children once they leave home. These plans will help to overcome some of the silence in our homes once the children are gone. My boys like to hunt and fish. I enjoy it, too, but I must confess that when I go fishing and hunting, I take a book and camera with me. I try to do this a lot with my boys. Chad likes to fish, so we plan at least one big fishing trip a year. Usually he and I go alone. Todd likes to hunt, and we plan one big hunting trip a year, usually just the two of us. I have a lot of pleasant, funny and happy memories of these trips. I wish I could tell you about them. Since I can't go into that in this book, just try to picture the smile I have on my face right now thinking about those trips. I have an agreement with Todd and Chad, that once they leave home we will continue to have that big trip together. This can be a good thing for you to do also. I expect these two trips will be the highlight of my life once they leave home. As a matter of fact, Todd and I will be going on a muzzleload hunt in a couple of weeks, and we are eagerly looking forward to it.

Another thing that would help you when the silence of an empty nest exists is to plan a special dinner during the holidays for your children and their families. At our home, we enjoy Thanksgiving more than any other holiday. We expect our family to be with us now, and once they leave home we want them to plan on coming home for this holiday. Since 1980 we have gone to a nursing home and invited a patient to spend Thanksgiving day with us. The person we bring home is not related to us at all. We just want a special person with us that day. We hope to continue this tradition for the rest of our lives. Why don't you try this and see why Jesus said it is more blessed to give than to receive (Acts 20:35). I believe it helps us more than it does the person who comes home with us for Thanksgiving.

I believe if we develop good habits now with our children, then once they leave home they will continue in them. Now is a good time to let them know that you want to continue certain activities even after they are on their own. This will let them know that they will always have a home to come back to. It will also make them *want* to come home again and again. I pray that my boys will keep my good habits and forget the bad ones. One good habit I have is what I am doing right now. I am sitting in a deer stand in the woods writing part of this book. Chad is about 100 yards away from me. He knows that I love him and want to be with him. He is so excited today. We have been here since 6:00 a.m. and haven't seen a deer yet, but we are having the time of our lives. I want him to develop this habit so he will do these things with his children. I would rather my boys be in the woods hunting any day than to be on the streets, driving a car, or getting into trouble. By the way, the reason Todd isn't with us today is because he got a deer two days ago. Boy, is he happy! It was his first one, and I'm so proud of him. I got a picture of it, and have shown it to everyone.

My two boys are not perfect, but I really love them. I hope they will develop good habits so they can share them with everyone they meet. If they do this, then when the home is silent Ruby and I will be content knowing that they are in good hands, and that their children are in good hands, also.

You Need To Renew Your Love For Each Other

It is said that many homes are destroyed once the children have left home. So many today are getting a divorce after 20-25 years of marriage together. Most lived their lives for their children and their jobs, having taken their mate for granted over all those years. They look at their lives and say, "We have nothing in common, so let's get a divorce." To that I say, "Hog-wash!" You have the rest of your lives to renew your love for each other. (Of course, it is best to work on this relationship every day of your marriage, rather than wait till this point, but even so, it is not too late to rekindle your love for one another).

I believe that before they leave home, the husband and wife need to do many things together without the children. Examples include eating out, shopping, movies, weekend trips without the children, etc. Think of common interests that you and your mate share that will keep you together now and once the children leave home. Then you will have all those activities in common. I told Ruby a long time ago that if she left me for another man after the children left us, then I would pack my bags and go with her, because I couldn't live without her. I hope you feel the same way about your mate. That was meant as a joke, but I couldn't imagine being without my Ruby.

I believe a good way to renew your love for each other after the children have left home is to think of all the things you did together before you were married. You will be surprised at how much more you will enjoy those activities now. I also believe that you will have as much fun doing them now, and possibly even more fun because you have the time and the experience to enjoy them now. Before you were married, and even after you were married, you were limited with time and money. Maybe now you have more of both. Or at least you have more time to do things and that is what it is all about. That is to use your time instead of abusing and wasting it. Time is so important that we don't have the right to waste any of it. God gave it to us and is giving it to us right now. I don't mean that you have to be busy doing something all the time, because even our time of relaxation is good for us, and we need it just as much as we need time to work.

I also suggest that you visit your friends and family more now than you ever did. Now that the children have left the nest, you have more time to visit them and others. A visit with people, even if it is a short visit, will help people more than you will ever know. Isn't it sad that we only realize how much of a short period of time we spent with our children once they have already grown up? I would say that all of us wish we had spent more time with our children than we did. We can't live our lives over and change that time. But we can start today spending time with them and try to be better parents now than we ever were. I'm sure that our children would like for us to have spent more time with them. But I believe that they could forget about the past if we are willing to spend more time with them *now*. By spending time with your children and others, it will help you as husband or wife, to appreciate what you have at home. And the whole purpose of spending time with others is to go and do things with your mate.

You Need A Hobby (Lots Of Them)

Now that your children have left the nest you *must* find a hobby. As a matter of fact, you should have found a hobby long before the time that your children are preparing to leave. Then you would have a head start on your new life without the children being home. There are so many hobbies in this world that I won't even begin to list them. There are many good works in your library, or in a book store that will give you some good ideas, so take advantage of them and start today.

The most rewarding hobby that you will ever undertake would be something that you can make which you can sell or give away. You will be surprised at how much money you can make just with a hobby. As a matter of fact many hobbies have ended up being a large business. If this happens, then accept it as a gift from God and start another hobby if you want to. Many people, especially family members, like the things you make more than the things you buy. It is just more special.

I suggest that you find some hobby that you and your mate can share together. The whole idea of an empty nest is for you and your mate to spend more enjoyable time together. And believe me, a hobby will do it. It is hard on your mate when you spend eight or ten hours a day in the garage, and she is in the house all alone. Sure, there are times when everyone needs to be alone, but there are more times when we need to be with each other!

I know that many congregations have a lot of things that a person could do which in a way is a hobby. Some congregations have quilting bees for the elderly; others make flowers for the hospital patients. There are many good things that they do, and you need to be a part of their good works. Some churches have a furniture repair shop. They fix up old furniture and give it away. What a great thing to do! So do you see why it is so important to have a work like this?

You Need The Church

I will be referring to this need of the church all through this book. This is the most important need that a person could ever have. I know most people think they don't need the church, but when it comes to the judgment day, they will regret not being a part of the church. Dear friend, don't wait until then. Get things right with God now so you will be ready to meet Him one day.

Once you have an empty nest, then you must fill that void with something else. I don't imagine you would want to start a family again. Going through dirty diapers and the whole thing of raising children just doesn't appeal to me at this point. So I suggest that if you are not a part of the family of God, then you need to be. We all need the family. As a matter of fact the whole purpose of this book is to help us have a better family life. The best family life that I know of is the church. In the church you have people who care for you. You have people who will cry with you and laugh with you. You have people who need each other. They need you just as much as you need them. When you miss a service of the church, you not only hurt yourself, but you hurt the church—those who love you and care for you. When the doors are open to the church building, I suggest that you be there and never miss a service of the church.

How sad it is to see people who are growing old and don't see the need of the church. If you are reading this book and are a part of the family of God, then keep it up. On the other hand, if you are reading this book and you don't see the need of the church being a part of your life, then you should put this book away and start reading your Bible. Because, dear friend, you are missing out on too much in this life, not to mention the life to come. I am convinced that you care about the church because I cannot imagine anyone who has a family (or who has already raised a family) not seeking after God's help. I don't believe that there will ever be a perfect family in this life. Even the best of families have problems. By the way, if your family is still at home, then give them time, not money. I have a chapter in this book about the church, so just remember you need the church and the church needs you.

Don't Stay Bored—Do Something!

This relates a little to your hobbies. Remember I said you need a hobby to keep you busy after the children have left home. Boredom is a tool of the devil. He uses his tool on more young people than he does us older ones. Yet at times we do get bored, so let me suggest some things to you that might help you to overcome boredom.

1. *GET OUT OF THE HOUSE.* The best way to overcome boredom is to get up from that couch and get out of the house. Some of the most pleasant times you and your mate will ever have is when you get in the car and start driving down the road, going nowhere. You are not going out to eat, you are not going to visit the children, you are not going to the store, you are not going shopping. As a matter of fact you are not going anywhere. Try this, even when you are not bored and it will make you realize what a good time you can have together. By doing this, you will be able to stop and smell the roses. You will notice things along the road that you never noticed before. You will see new houses that have been there for years. I believe that we don't have to have a purpose for everything we do. The spur of the moment events are very rewarding.

2. *GO VISIT PEOPLE.* The main people that you need to visit are your children. Maybe you can visit them too much, but I'll bet they will be glad to see you come over. While you are there, don't give them a lot of advice, unless they ask you for it. They need to make their own decisions and sometimes they need to learn from their own mistakes. Don't you agree?

Another group of people you need to visit are the elderly who are a part of your congregation. They welcome visits. They don't get too many, and it is sad that once we get old, people and family tend to forget about our needs. So if you want to overcome boredom and you want to cheer someone up, then go and visit an older person, okay?

3. *GO SHOPPING.* You don't have to spend any money, just go to a local mall and look around. I'll tell you something that I like to do around the holidays. I like to go to a large mall and watch people. I tell Ruby to shop and come back in an hour or so and get me. She loves that, and I get to sit down with an ice cream cone and just watch people. People amaze me during the holidays. I am sure they look at me and say "Look at that weird man just sitting there eating ice cream." But, dear friend, I have seen it all by just sitting there watching people. I like to say "hello" to people every now and then as they go by. It will surprise you how they react. Some wonder why you spoke; some ignore you. Some will frown; some will smile. Some will even come back later and say "hello" to you. And if someone sits next to me, then look out, because my goal is to have them smiling within one minute. I love people, and you need to love them, too. If you are ever in a mall around Cleveland or Chattanooga, Knoxville, or Cookeville, Tennessee, or Atlanta, Georgia, then look for me around the holidays. I will be the good-looking man with the ice cream sitting there looking at you. If you see me, then come by and say hello. If that isn't me, what have you lost? At least you are not bored.

4. *COOK SOMETHING.* I love to cook and when I want to do something, I begin to get out the recipe books. Ruby and I love to make candy and give it to other people. She has just lost 32 pounds and I lost 20 pounds, so we don't eat much candy. Cooking will take your mind off being bored or being alone. The best thing about cooking is you can reap of your own laborers. Many colleges have classes on cooking. Take a course and learn how to cook new things. I might say more about this later, but now I think I will go and fry me some Tennessee fried chicken. Boy, can I fry and eat Tennessee fried chicken!

Help Other People—(especially those with children)

One of the best ways to solve the empty nest problem is to get out of the house and help people. We live in a world today where we don't want to help one another. We think that we are self-sufficient, and we can do everything without anyone else. If the world thinks that, then it is up to you and me to change their attitude. I believe that once you lend a helping hand to someone, then you are also helping yourself. It is a good feeling to know that you are helping someone.

At this point in your life you have the greatest opportunity to help others that you will ever have. Your children have left home and you have time on your hands to share with other people, especially those raising young children. You can pet them and send them home afterwards. Before, you could not do that. If you are a grandparent, then you need to take advantage of that opportunity. Children are people who need love from everyone, and you are the one who must show them love.

When it comes to helping other people, then this is where you need to put your mind to work You need to sit around looking for things to do. Once you think of things to do, then write them down and go over your list often. If possible, put those things on a counter and do different things to help people during the month. Another good way is to put down people's names on the calendar, and do things for them, even if it is only a call on their birthday. They will appreciate it very much.

Helping The Empty Nest To Be A Great Place To Live

Some people think that the empty nest is the worst place to be in life. Well, I disagree with them because I believe that the worst place to be is to be dead. With this in mind, we must look at the good things in life and the good things in an empty nest. When a husband and wife are at home alone, it takes both of them working together to make life worth living. There will be times when one won't want to do something with the other. I believe that you need to force yourself, and if possible, go ahead and do those things with your mate. By forcing yourself to do things, then most of the time you will end up having a good time, and you will be happy because you did it. It will be sort of like a snowball—the more you roll it, the bigger it gets. I believe that life is that way, because the more we do things with other people, the more we will like it.

Many times what makes an empty nest great is that you can eat, sleep, play and work when you want to. That is a privilege that very few of us are able to enjoy. The main thing about this privilege is not to abuse it. If you sit up most of the night watching T.V. and sleep most of the day, then, my dear friend, you will miss out on life. If you find yourself in this type of situation, then stop it right away. If you are like this, then it won't take long until you will put on extra weight, you will get lazy, you will develop a negative attitude, you will stay tired, and feel you are not getting enough rest. I feel so sorry for those who have to work all night and sleep all day. I believe that God made day for us to work and night for us to rest. It is a shame that this world thinks it must produce things twenty-four hours a day. I wish that no factory or business was open all night. I also wish that nothing was open on Sunday. This way we could have more time at home with our family. If you can control your hours, then by all means don't waste them. Use those hours for the glory of God.

You have spent many years providing for your family. Now that the two (or one) of you are home alone, begin to do things that you could not do while your children were home. To make an empty nest great, you must *do* something. If you just sit around or lie around all the time, you will never have a "great" empty nest. Develop some good reading habits. That will help you a lot. I would suggest that you read and study the Bible every day. If you do this, you will learn new things every day. Now is also a good time to become a Bible school teacher. You have the time to study. You can gain the knowledge and the wisdom to do a great job. I believe that if you are not teaching, then you are doing the church and God an injustice. You now have the ability to do so, because of your spare time!

The Empty Nest

1. Explain the need to plan for retirement years before the time arrives.

2. Why is it important to realize that the children aren't coming home to live again?

3. What are some good things that you can make for your children?

4. What will make our children want to come home for regular visits?

5. How can you renew your love for your spouse?

6. Why are hobbies necessary when one finds himself with "an empty nest?"

7. Discuss the role the church plays with those facing an empty nest.

8. How can the empty nest help other people?

SUFFERING AND THE DEATH
OF A LOVED ONE

Suffering And The Death Of A Loved One

T he reason for this chapter is because of a good friend named Judy who has a husband who is very ill. She told me that I should write a book about suffering and death. I told her I was writing one on the family and that I would include a chapter in it about suffering. After I began this study, I realized that a book about the family would be incomplete if it did not include such a chapter. Every family eventually has suffering and death to overcome at one time or another. This whole book has been positive in nature. I wanted you to smile while you read this book. And this chapter will be no exception. I know that you may be saying, "That's ridiculous!" But finish this chapter before you make a decision on it, okay? I realize that you will probably shed tears while reading this chapter, and maybe you will shed tears while reading the rest of the book. Don't feel alone. I have shed many tears over some things that are in this book—things which have happened to me and to others whom I love. It hurts me when others hurt, but maybe if we can all help people smile and look at the good in things, then we can make this a little better world in which to live. In this chapter I will be using a lot of names of people who are friends or acquaintances of mine. I have their permission to do so, but I am leaving off their last names for various reasons. Some of these people are, and were, great heroes of mine.

I will tell you about Judy in a minute, but first let me tell you about a man whom I loved very much. He was a hero to me. His name was Wayne. I guess you know by reading this that he is now deceased. But let me tell you about his life before we talk about his sickness. The reason I can smile even though he is gone, is that Wayne was a friend to everyone. Since his death, I have talked to many people who claimed Wayne as their friend. They told me he taught their Bible class, how he performed their wedding ceremony, how he always had kind words for everyone, how he loved people, and a thousand other kind things about him. You see why I can smile? It's because of the good influence he had on me and others. Oh, I'm not saying he was perfect, but name one person living today who is. As a matter of fact, I only know of one person who ever lived in this world that was perfect, and that was Jesus Christ.

The best thing that I liked about Wayne was that I could talk to him, and he would give me his undivided attention. And many people whom I talk to still tell me that he would listen to them. He was a great listener. Not only would he listen to me and others, but he would try his best to do something about what you told him. This makes me smile today. You see, if we can remember the good that people leave behind, then it should put a smile on our faces.

I remember once I told Wayne that I like grapes. He got me five grape vines, and I get grapes from them every year. Boy, those are the best grapes I have ever had! As long as those grapevines are alive, then Wayne will be alive to me. I take special care of them, for I want them to be here when I am gone. I think more of those grapevines than anything. Wayne knew that if I had wanted to, I could have bought a vineyard. But he also knew how to touch my heart, and the hearts of others. Every time I eat any of those grapes, and every time I give grapes to people, I think of Wayne and I tell them who gave them to me. You know, a person would be a fool not to accept $1,000 for each of those vines, but I wouldn't take a million dollars for each one. That would be five million dollars! Now I'm sure you are saying, "Bill, you are lying, because you know you would take that for the grape vines. You could buy a million vines for that price, and have a great vineyard." Dear friend, I am very serious. Money cannot buy those grape vines, That, my dear friend, is how much I loved Wayne, and still love his dear wife.

The good thing about Wayne was that he was a faithful Christian. Another good thing about him is that his wife, son, and his son's family are faithful Christians. The early church had a tradition that I wish we had today. When a Christian died, they would all dress up in white to show that they could smile because a Christian had laid down his burdens and gone to a better place. If we did that today, then we would have worn white to brother Wayne's funeral.

Now, on a sad note, let me tell you a little about Wayne's sickness. While in bed, sick for a few months, I could see Wayne fading away every time I visited him. I would talk to him about the church. He would always tell us how people had been calling and visiting him. He would tell me of the love he had for the church. He would tell me what a great wife he had, and how she took care of him. He always told me that he was ready to leave this life. I hope I will be ready when I die, don't you?

It may be that you at this very time have a loved one who is sick or dying with cancer like Wayne. To you, I can only say that I don't know why this happens. I don't know why evil people live through horrible car accidents, while a good person can stick a nail in his foot and die like my grandfather did. I'm not saying that I want some people to die and not others. I am saying that I don't know why this happens. And neither does anyone else. But we must look beyond suffering and death, for many people are suffering much more than we are. Look around, or go with me some time to the hospital and look at those people, and it will make us appreciate what we have in life.

Finally, to me, Wayne was the good Samaritan, as recorded in Luke 10:25-37. He will always be in my heart and the hearts of so many others. Our hearts can rejoice because he is at a better place than we are. We will still suffer, still be tempted, still do things wrong, still cry, still have pain, and still suffer death. But you know none of those things will ever bother Wayne again. Here is what the Bible says about Wayne, and people like him:

"And I saw a new heaven and a new earth: for the first heaven and the first earth were passed away; and there was no more sea, and I John saw the holy city, new Jerusalem, coming down from God out of heaven saying, Behold the tabernacle of God is with men, and he will dwell with them, and they shall be his people, and God himself shall be with them, and be their God. And God shall wipe away all tears from their eyes; and there shall be no more death, neither sorrow, nor crying, neither shall there be any more pain; for the former things are passed away." (Revelation 21:1-4)

Judy

Judy is like many of us today. She is a friend to many people. Many love and respect her. She has a very good attitude toward life. She cares for other people. She is always asking me how my family is doing, and I appreciate that very much. She has two wonderful children whom I think very highly of. She has a wonderful husband that is respected by many. He is like Judy; he cares for people. I think a lot of him, and so do his friends. He has helped me in making the decision to spend more time at home and less time at work. He always asks me if I'm still taking more time off from work. He cares for me and shows it with his concern.

Now you might be saying, "Well, this family is better off than my own family, so what is the big deal about Judy?" Well, Judy is hurting. Her husband has a chronic disease and will probably never get better. Just in the past month he had to take a medical retirement from work. I'm sure this hurts him a lot. The hurting Judy is going through is watching her husband suffer. This has got to be one of the hardest things a husband or wife can go through. To see a loved one's health go down every day is very hard to take. Many like Judy are saying, "Why is this happening to us? Why do sinful people seem to have no problems, and we are trying to do what's right and are suffering so much?"

To answer these questions and others is very hard. But at the end of this chapter I will set aside a few pages to discuss suffering and death in more detail. I will try to give you some answers that I hope will help all of us.

Now, back to Judy. I wanted to mention her in order to give you some examples of how people are hurting all around us. We need to listen to things that people are saying because maybe we can help them in some way. But if we only think of ourselves, then we won't have time for Judy and others like her. God forbid that we ever get to the point where we don't have time to listen.

Now, let me mention a few other people before we get into some ways of handling suffering and death.

Linda And Martha

It is so strange. About a year ago Martha and Linda developed cancer in their bodies and are very critically ill at the time this is being written. These two ladies are heroines of mine. They have accepted their fate and seem to understand more about this life than I will ever understand. The most impressive thing about these two women is that they continue to come to worship services. It is a great encouragement to me and others to see them. At times, when I talk to them, I can hardly hold back the tears. I and others are daily praying for them. Each week they take treatment, and it is so hard on them. They get sick and very weak. I am sure most of us know about this, but I want you to see how people all around us are hurting. The challenge we have is whether or not we are willing to help these people. And I hope we accept the challenge and give it the best we possibly can.

Isn't it amazing that people like Linda and Martha were so faithful before their sickness began, and that they remain faithful to God? Many people who might have a toenail hurting are not able to make it to church services. You know there is true dedication when someone is so ill they have to breathe with the assistance of an oxygen tank, and they bring the tank along and continue to attend services. I know there are days when we don't feel like going to worship. I also know that many of us have gone to services when we were sick and feeling bad, and maybe when we should have been at home. But it hurts me when we make up excuses, and people like Linda and Martha still hang in there. I expect by this time this book is ready for publication that these two saints won't be with us.

To the families of these two saints, I wish I had some words of wisdom that would immediately help you to overcome all of your suffering. You see, we all know that the family suffers a great deal while their loved one is dying. I hope that by the end of this chapter I will be able to give you some comfort. The only problem is that there is no miracle cure for those who are hurting. But I believe through the scriptures, loved ones, and good books, we can find a little relief. I have noticed each time that I visit these ladies they always ask about the condition of the other. Plus, they always ask how our families are doing, and how other members of the congregation are. I take great honor in this because that shows me that they care for other people. Probably if I were in their shoes I would not be thinking of others, but would instead want everyone to be interested more in me. But not these two lovely ladies. They have hearts of gold, and it is causing me to shed tears as I write this about them. I pray that if I ever get sick like they are, (and who knows, all of us might be there one day), that I will have the same attitude about people and life and death as they do. They can smile even through their suffering. They can laugh even though it hurts them. If they can be this way, then can't all of us who have our health be a little more happy and smile with them?

Martin

Martin was one of only about five people that I have ever met in my lifetime who while he was well and getting around pretty good would tell me that he was ready to die and looked forward to the day when he could go and be with the Lord. I can understand it when some people every now and then tell me they are ready to leave this life. But to Martin it was a goal that he wanted to accomplish. Since he felt that way while he was in pretty good health, just imagine how he felt while he was sick and dying. I loved visiting him. He would always tell me of how much he loved the church. He always asked us to pray for him while we were there. And he wanted us to pray for him in our daily prayers. He was a man who believed in prayer. Although he could hardly walk, couldn't hear very well, and had many other ailments, I don't know that he really wanted us to pray for his health. I felt he wanted us to pray that the Lord would come quickly and relieve him of his suffering. As a matter of fact, he told us that on many occasions. I remember how he loved to talk about wrestling. Boy, he sure was enthusiastic about it. I can see his smile now as he discussed it. Now, if Martin could have an attitude of comfort, contentment in the state he was in, then don't you think that all of us could have a better outlook on life?

I believe that Martin could see what I want to see and what I'm encouraging you to see, and that is that we are just passing through this land, this is not our home. We are here for a visit, and that visit will determine where our home will be after this life. While here we have to do right and help others along the way. We don't have much time on this visit, so we have to make good use of the time. We are only pilgrims passing through.

Now before I close this section on Martin, I am going to make one exception to this chapter. I'm going to mention a saint whom I love and who helped Martin so much. I chose not to mention people's names in this chapter in order to protect them from different things that we don't need to know about. But in this case I am sure Martin would want me to mention her. Her name is Pearl. She is a "pearl" of great price. I can remember when Martin was beginning to lose his health, and it seemed that not very many people were around to help him. I am sorry to say that even the church didn't go out of its way to help him, and I feel so sad about that. But the only person I can blame for this is myself. I should have done more for him. Now it seems that when no one seems to care, God raises up someone who does. That was Pearl. She did everything that was possible for him. He never wanted for anything as long as he was with her. I guess she took care of him for over two years. Many would not do that for two days. But Pearl is someone who cares and wants to give her best. You know, within those two years Martin converted her to Christ and she is now a faithful Christian.

Isn't it amazing how God works through people? I think back to that year. Martin could barely walk, was hard of hearing, and had many other ailments. Feeling very bad at times, going through a lot of pain, and yet he converted Pearl to Christ. That year I was, and still am, in perfect health and did not convert anyone to Christ. What is it? Do you and I have to suffer affliction before we can care about the souls of people? I hope not. So I hope you can take courage in Martin and be more like him in that way. I also hope that we can realize that all of us can be a "Pearl" in this life. We just need to care for people and begin to do something about it. God is looking for a "Martin" and a "Pearl" today. Won't we let him find it in us?

Loretta

I remember about 10 years ago I was asked to go to the hospital to visit a lady that was dying and was in very bad condition. When I arrived there I didn't know who in the world she was. All I knew was that she had smoked all her life. The doctors took out one of her lungs and part of the other because of her lung cancer. When I saw her I thought, "Why do people smoke and destroy their lives?" I thought "Didn't she know that there are so many things in life that can kill us, and we don't need to deliberately do something that will hurt us?" I felt like I couldn't really love anyone who was like this. I was wrong. I'm sure I will be wrong many other times.

After Loretta got out of the hospital, for three years I visited her and her husband every Tuesday night. I remember the hot chocolate and cookies that they would always treat me to. Within those three years we converted both of them to Christ and developed a mother and father relationship with them. They were old enough to be our grandparents and we really fell in love with them. So did the church. They were always doing good for the church, and for others. Loretta's husband has now passed away, but she is still doing well. I didn't expect her to live for a month when I first met her, and now it has been over ten years. Am I thankful to God for her.

You see, we don't know what God has in mind for us. He might take our life today, or we might live for a long period of time. So the challenge to us is, if we are sick, or if we have a loved one who is sick, then we need to look at the good in everything and give it our best. Loretta is still serving God and we must do the same thing.

Why Is There Suffering?

Now let's talk a little about suffering. I am sure some of you are saying, "Why didn't he talk about this in the beginning of the last chapter?" I wanted to let you know that there are other people who suffer besides yourself. I hope it made you realize that if you are alive, then be thankful, for there is still hope.

Suffering is something that I believe we all must go through. It is something that I believe at times we need. Let me mention some things about suffering that might help us.

1. We Need Suffering
2. We Can't Escape Suffering
3. Others Suffer More Than We Do
4. We Can't Understand Everything About Suffering

We Need Suffering

I'll bet you are tempted to lay this book down right now, because of the title of this section. I also suppose some of you closed the book up and left it for a few days because you disagree with me on this point. I have done the same thing to books I've read. But when I come back to them, I get a lot of good ideas. Now the reason I said that we need suffering is that we could never appreciate the sunshine if we didn't have rain. How could we appreciate summer if we didn't have winter? How could we appreciate a new car if we didn't have an old one? How could we appreciate a steak if we didn't have beans? You see whre all this leads to. I could give you a hundred examples, but I think you get the point.

If everyone were healthy all the time, then we would never appreciate good health. We could never have mercy or compassion for people if we had never been in their shoes. When anyone tells me about his head hurting, I want to cry for him, because I get migraines about twice a month. Some of them will last for two days. I try not to let people know that I have a headache because unless you have had a migraine before, you could not know what it is like. I can be in bed with a wet towel over my face, and I can hear people breathe in the next room, and it makes the pain worse. Ruby and the boys are very considerate of me when I get a headache and they leave me alone. You see, what I'm trying to say is that when we are sick, in the hospital or at home, we really think about God, family, and our health. But if we go through life without pain, then I believe that most of us would not take time to examine our lives. If we don't take that time, then we will be very disappointed when we stand before God on the judgment day.

I realize that when we are suffering, we think "Why does this happen to me?" I wouldn't want anyone to have my pain, but I wish I didn't have it. But you know, *every time* I recover from a headache, I feel lke a new person. I want to shout and tell the world how good I feel. Before that migraine, I never wanted to shout and tell the world how good I felt, even though I felt as good before as I did after the headache. Another problem we have with suffering is that we think that we are the only one in the world who has pain. We also think that our pain is more severe than that of anyone else. Let me assure you that people had pain before we were born, and they will have pain after we are dead if the Lord tarries that long. I don't know of anyone in this world who does not have some type of pain. As a matter of fact, I have a doctor friend who told me that it is normal for us to have some type of pain, sooner or later.

Another thing about pain is that we can always find someone else who is suffering more than we are. I am sure you have heard the story of the man who complained he had no shoes until he saw a man with no feet. Sometimes we need to see other suffer before we can appreciate what we have. Now I know some of you are suffering right now, because you have a loved one who is sick or dying, or maybe even have experienced death in your family. To you I can only say that I hurt with you. I know how you feel. I know you need someone to talk to. I know you need to cry. I know you feel like giving up. I know that you feel like all is lost. I have been there. But let me assure you that if things don't get any better in this life, then a Christian won't have any suffering in the life to come. Doesn't that make you want to smile? Go ahead and smile, because you can have that great reward of heaven one day. I hope that you can now understand that through suffering, all of us can be better people, and I believe that we can say that it was good for us to suffer because we needed it.

We Can't Get Away From It

Suffering and death are two things that we cannot get away from. I don't know of anyone who has not suffered in some form or another, and all us are going to die, unless we are alive when the Lord returns. The problem we have with suffering and death is that we think it will not happen to us. If we could only change our thinking on this subject, then I believe we can face suffering, and even death, with dignity. The more I suffer and the longer I live, I try to understand suffering more and more. I don't believe that God causes us to suffer. I believe that our body was not designed to live forever here on this earth. That is the reason why we suffer, and eventually die. But I also believe that God gives us some type of wisdom when we are suffering, in order to prepare us for death. Let us explain it to you this way. When we, or a loved one, suffers, and even approaches death, that gives us time to make plans for the future whether we are alive or dead. While we are in good health and everything is going well, most of us don't take time to prepare for life or death. But once we are on our back due to illness, then we have a different outlook on life.

I believe that we could live to be 100 years old and still not be ready to die. There is something about living that we want to hang on to just as long as possible. I, for one, want to live to be 100 years old. But I also must prepare myself to meet death at any time. The most important way to prepare for death is to become a Christian. If you are not a Christian, then my friend, you are not prepared for anything. May I encourage you to become a Christian and to remain a faithful Christian for the rest of your life. You will then be prepared for death, whenever it comes. Read these scriptures: Mark 16:16; Romans 10:10; Acts 2:38; Romans 6; Galatians 3:27; Acts 10; Acts 16.

Once your mind accepts suffering and even death, then we can have a better outlook upon life. If we could only realize that we are only going to be here for a short time but will be in the life to come for eternity, then we could exert better control of the life we now live. And before we even get sick, we can live a controlled life to prepare ourselves for the life to come. To me, it is harder to see a loved one suffer than to suffer myself. But we all will suffer, and we cannot get away from that. We need to look to the Bible to find comfort for ourselves and for others.

Others Suffer More Than We Do

I realize that when we suffer, we think that we are alone. That no one else suffers. I also realize that we forget about everyone else and concentrate on our own problems. I know that when my head hurts really bad, I really don't care about anyone else's pain. Also, when a loved one dies, we are hurting so badly that we can't think about anyone else. Now maybe this is part of our problem. We are so concerned with ourselves that we don't take time to think about others. Don't get me wrong, I believe that when we suffer (and especially when a loved one suffers or dies), we need to shed tears. I would rather cry for a loved one any day than to ignore his pain. The Bible teaches us to weep with those who weep. But you know, we are so blessed in this country that we need to be thankful every day for our blessings. If we could only look around us, then we could see people who suffer much more than we do. And we can also see people who have less than we have.

I don't know anything about medicine, and I'm sure most doctors would disagree with my next statement. But I believe we could overcome a lot of pain and suffering if we could only accept it and go on through life with a smile. You are probably saying, "How can I smile when I'm sick?" Dear friend, there are a lot of people in life who smile even when they are suffering. They have a positive outlook on life. We all need to have that type of outlook. Now I'm not saying that we should never complain about our pain. I am saying that the more we complain about it, the more it hurts. And the more we complain, the less people want to listen, or be around us. When I have a migraine, I want to complain, and I want sympathy. But when I have an ordinary headache, I usually don't even tell anyone about it.

Now concerning the death of a loved one, I know how you feel, for I have been there. A few people can never overcome the death of a loved one. It *is* very difficult. It always bothers me when people say, "Don't cry" or "Don't let it bother you - life must go on." I like to tell people to go ahead and cry, and *let* it bother them, because that loved one's life has ended here. But the good news is that a Christian lives after death with God! I don't think we should ever forget a loved one who has died. I don't mean that we should dwell on it day and night, but I believe that we should always keep a place in our heart and mind for them. My mother was killed in an automobile accident 25 years ago, and I still like to remember the good things she did for us. I smile when I think of some of those events. She loved us more than any one I have ever known in this life. I would give all I have today just to spend one hour with her right now. I'm shedding tears now, but I also realize that my mind and heart can spend time with her, so that gives me great joy and allows me to smile again.

I hope you can see what I see when it comes to pain and suffering. I believe it is mostly a state of mind, and we need to control our mind so we can have a good attitude on life. And I believe this will help us to live longer.

Finally, let me say one more thing about pain, suffering, and death. You have got to be a Christian because if not, then you cannot overcome anything in this life. And you sure won't be able to overcome anything in the life to come. How can anyone face pain, or death, without knowing that he is safe in God's hands? As a matter of fact, how can anyone who is in perfect health go to sleep without knowing that if he died, he would not be with Jesus? Dear friend, if you don't know that, then you had better not close your eyes until you have made everything right with God.

Read the following scriptures: Mark 16:16; Luke 13:3; Romans 10:10 and Matthew 28:18-20.

We Can't Understand Everything About Suffering

It doesn't matter how many books we read about suffering. It doesn't matter how much we see people suffer. It doesn't matter how much we suffer. We just cannot understand everything about suffering. It is true that we can learn a lot on the subject. And we should all try to understand more about it. I guess one who is really able to understand the most is the person who has experienced the same pain. I'm sure you have noticed that when someone mashes a finger, or something minor like that, it's sometimes funny to us. But that person is in pain. My dad and I work together a lot, and when I drop a board on his toe, I laugh, or when he runs into me with a 2 x 4, he laughs. The victim is in pain! So you see what I mean when I say that you need to suffer to understand the pain of others. Now I'm not saying that you should cause yourself pain so that you can understand pain. I don't have to put my hand into a fire to know that it will burn me. But what I am saying is that when we try to comfort people and we haven't suffered their type of pain, then just tell them so, but tell them that we are there to help in any way we can.

Suffering is something that affects all of us differently. But one thing for sure is that it affects all of us. You can look at a family, who from outward appearances seems to have no problems or suffering, but I feel sure that they suffer, or have suffered, just as we do. You see, as long as we live in this world, we will have suffering and problems. The thing for us to do is to accept it and realize that the alternative to suffering is to die. I would rather have problems and suffering now than to die today, wouldn't you?

Finally, let me say that there is coming a day when there will be no more pain, problems, or suffering. When that days comes, those of us who are Christians will do away with all of this and have a new home in heaven. I want that home, don't you? The only way we can have that home is to prepare for it in this life. Are you preparing for that home? I hope so. If not, then won't you start today with your family and gain the family of the saved one day?

Suffering And The Death Of A Loved One

1. Explain the importance of a smile when people are suffering.

2. Will our example live on after we are no longer here?

3. What does the faithful Christian have to look forward to after suffering and death?

4. What can we do to help people who have a mate, children, or parents who are seriously ill?

5. How can we help those who are sick?

6. Explain why those who are on their deathbed understand life and death so much better than we do.

7. Discuss Hebrews 11:13.

Credits

1. "Building Stronger Families"
   by Royce Money
   Victor Books, Wheaton, Illinois 60187

2. "Happiness In The Home"
   by Harold Hazelip
   Baker Book House, Grand Rapids, Michigan 49506

3. "Hide and Seek"
   by Dr. James Dobson
   Power Books, Old Tappan, New Jersey

4. "Parents In Pain"
   by John White
   Inter Varsity Press, Downers Grove, Illinois 60515

5. "The Strong-Willed Child"
   by Dr. James Dobson
   Tynale House Publishers, Inc., Wheaton, Illinois

6. "Where Have All The Mothers Gone"
   by Brenda Hunter
   Zonderman Publishing House, Grand Rapids, Michigan

7. "Communications"
   by H. Norman Wright
   Regal Books, Ventura California

Though I read over 100 books before beginning this one, the books cited above are the primary ones in preparing this manuscript.